Sir Walter Ralegh
and the
New World

Sir Walter Ralegh and the New World

John W. Shirley

Raleigh
America's Four Hundredth Anniversary Committee
North Carolina Department of Cultural Resources

America's Four Hundredth Anniversary Committee

Lindsay C. Warren, Jr.
Chairman

Marc Basnight
Andy Griffith
John P. Kennedy
Robert V. Owens, Jr.

William S. Powell
L. Richardson Preyer
S. Thomas Rhodes
Harry Schiffman
Mrs. J. Emmett Winslow

David Stick
Mrs. Percy Tillett
Charles B. Wade, Jr.
Charles B. Winberry, Jr.

John D. Neville
Executive Director

Mrs. Marsden B. deRosset, Jr.
Assistant Director

Advisory Committee on Publications

William S. Powell
Chairman

Lindley S. Butler
Jerry C. Cashion
David Stick
Alan D. Watson

Contents

Maps and Illustrations

Foreword

America's Four Hundredth Anniversary Committee, formed in 1978 under the provisions of an act of the North Carolina General Assembly of 1973, was charged with recommending plans for the observance of the quadricentennial of the first English attempts to explore and settle North America. The committee has proposed to carry out a variety of programs to appeal to a broad range of people. Among these is a publications program that includes a series of booklets dealing with the history of the events and people of the 1580s.

Queen Elizabeth I of England enjoyed a reign that was for the most part peaceful. It was a period of prosperity, which saw the flourishing of a new interest in literature, religion, exploration, and business. English mariners began to venture farther from home, and in time talk began to be heard of hopes to establish naval bases and colonies in America. Men of the County of Devon in the southwest of England, seafarers for generations, played leading roles in this expansion. One of these, Walter Ralegh (as he most often wrote his name), became a favorite of the queen, and on him she bestowed a variety of honors and rewards. It was he to whom she granted a charter in 1584 authorizing the discovery and occupation of lands not already held by "any Christian Prince and . . . people." Ralegh promptly sent a reconnaissance expedition to what is now North Carolina, and this was followed in due time by a colony under the leadership of Ralph Lane. Headquarters were established on Roanoke Island. After remaining for nearly a year and exploring far afield, Lane and his men returned to England in 1586.

In the summer of 1587 Governor John White and a colony of 115 men, women, and children arrived and occupied the houses and the fort left by Lane. The brief annals of this colony are recorded in a journal kept by the governor; they tell of certain problems that arose early—but they also record the birth of the first English child in America. The journal further explains why Governor White consented to return to England for supplies. His departure was the last contact with the settlers who constituted the "Lost Colony," renowned in history, literature, and folklore.

Although a casual acquaintance with the facts of these English efforts might suggest that they were failures, such was far from the case. Ralegh's expenditures of time, effort, and resources (in which he was joined by many others, including Queen Elizabeth herself) had salutary effects for England and certainly for all of present-day America. From Ralegh's initial investment in the reconnaissance voyage, as well as from the colonies, came careful descriptions of the New World and samples of its products. The people of England, indeed of the Western world, learned about North America; because books were published based on what Ralegh's men discovered, they could soon read for themselves of the natives there and the promise of strange and wonderful new resources.

From these voyages and colonizing efforts came the conviction that an English nation could be established in America. In 1606, when another charter was about to be issued for further settlement, King James, who succeeded Queen Elizabeth at her death in 1603, called for advice from some of the men who had been associated with Ralegh. They assured the king that further efforts would surely succeed. With this the Virginia Company was chartered, and it established England's first permanent settlement in America at Jamestown.

Because of Sir Walter Ralegh's vision, England persisted. Because of England's persistence and its refusal to yield to Spain's claims to the region, the United States today enjoys an English heritage. The English common law is the basis of American law; American legislative bodies are modeled on the House of Commons with the rights and freedoms that it developed over a long period of time; America's mother tongue is English, and it is the most commonly spoken language in the world—pilots and navigators on international airlines and the controllers who direct them at airports all over the world use English. Americans also share England's literary tradition: Chaucer, Beowulf, King Arthur, and Shakespeare are America's too, and Americans can enjoy Dickens and Tennyson, as well as Agatha Christie and Dorothy Sayers. America's religious freedom is also in the English tradition, and several of this nation's Protestant denominations trace their earliest history to origins in England: the Episcopal church, certainly, but the Quakers, Baptists, Congregationalists, and Universalists as well.

America's Four Hundredth Anniversary Committee has planned many programs to direct national and even international attention to the significance of events that occurred from bases established by English men, women, and children, but notably Sir Walter Ralegh, in what is now North Carolina during the period 1584-1590. While some of the programs may be regarded as fleeting and soon forgotten, the publications are intended to serve as lasting reminders of America's indebtedness to England. Books, pamphlets, and folders covering a broad range of topics have been prepared by authors on both sides of the Atlantic. These, it is anticipated, will introduce a vast new audience to the facts of America's origins.

Lindsay C. Warren, Jr., *Chairman*
America's Four Hundredth Anniversary Committee

I. England under the Tudors

The sixteenth century saw the adolescence of England as a nation. It was during that period that the nation changed, almost unwillingly, from a provincial, insular kingdom into a world power. When Christopher Columbus sailed into the unknown Atlantic, the British Isles were remote outposts lying on the fringes of the commercial world. But with the opening of the new sea-lanes and the advent of exciting traffic to the newfound lands to the west, Britain finally found itself in the center of an Atlantic-based economy that offered opportunities for trade in both Europe and the New World.

There was need for expansion of the British economic base. Populations were rising rapidly, from slightly more than 2 million in 1500 to more than 3¾ million by the end of the century. And in spite of the ravages of the plague and the new disease known as syphilis, which was brought from America by Spaniards, the population of Europe was also expanding. Greater demands for essential materials and foodstuffs led to shortages, gave to the emerging merchant class new incentives to expand their activities, and increased the availability of capital to invest in hopes of future profits. The opening of markets in the East had led to more luxuries for the general public than ever before and a standard of living for the wealthy undreamed of by previous generations. From the West came an abundance of fish offered by new fishing waters off Newfoundland, Iceland, and Greenland; these fish would form the staple of the diet of the masses. And the gold of the Aztecs and Incas, which the Spanish Plate Fleet was bringing to European coffers from Mexico and Peru, was changing the power base of Europe.

These fresh opportunities led English entrepreneurs to embark on commercial oceanic enterprises that in turn led step by step to the development of a notable nation and the evolution of an empire. King Henry VIII, shrewd Welshman that he was, recognized these potentials. Not only did he start to build a royal navy, but he also encouraged the exploration and piracy that would flourish under his daughter, Elizabeth I, and adopted new Italian bookkeeping methods to assure the crown of its share of any profits. Elizabeth, of the same stamp

Elizabeth I presided over a nation on the threshold of wealth, fame, and power. She was the focus of all attention during her reign, and upon her goodwill Sir Walter Ralegh came to depend. Engraving from copy in North Carolina Collection, University of North Carolina Library, Chapel Hill.

as her father, similarly believed in filling the coffers of the throne by expanding the nation's sea resources and was determined to secure the royal percentages due her treasury (although she was extremely cautious about investing her own capital in such ventures). As a result, growth in sea activities during her reign was almost logarithmic. Whereas at the death of Henry VIII there were but a score of sea masters competent to sail out of sight of land, by the time Queen Elizabeth died (1603), English seamen had twice circumnavigated the globe; probed the oceans of both polar regions; established and maintained commerce with Russia, India, Persia, and Japan; and vanquished both major naval powers—Spain and Portugal—in battles at sea. During the ensuing quarter century they would establish permanent colonies in Virginia, Massachusetts, and the sugar islands of the West Indies. Britain had assumed the role of mistress of the seas, and the British Empire had been founded.

This explosive physical world furnished opportunities for rapid acquisition of wealth, fame, and power never before available to the gentle or plebeian classes of Britain. And these opportunities were quickly seized by a people who were themselves somewhat adolescent and impetuous. It was during these years that the English character was forming: the native ebullience of the original Celts (still reasonably pure in the outlying districts of Ireland, Scotland, and Wales) was fusing with the stolid and methodical persistence of the Teutonic Angles, Saxons, and Jutes who had first conquered them; and a veneer of urbane and legalistic sophistication was superimposed upon all of them by the Normans. All of these traits were evident in the common citizen of that century, with strong national qualities being forged by the nationalistic fervor of King Henry and his daughter, Elizabeth Tudor. This fervor produced a nation of Englishmen that, during the following century, would become a world power. Although the Elizabethans have been called "a nest of singing birds," and although they produced poetry, drama, music, and art that entranced later generations in all countries, the real heroes to the aspiring youth of the sixteenth century were not the Spensers, Shakespeares, Marlowes, or Jonsons but the hardy and militant old sea dogs—the Cabots, Frobishers, Gilberts, Drakes, Grenvilles, Davises, and Newports.

The glory and greatest extravagance of this burgeoning and dynamic society was the court. There, during the last half of the century, Elizabeth the Virgin Queen maintained an assemblage of splendor and nobility new to the English people. In addition to her established counselors and ministers—William Cecil, Lord Burghley, the lord treasurer; his son, Robert Cecil, the earl of Salisbury, who was to succeed him; Sir Francis Walsingham, Elizabeth's principal secretary and head of her spy service; Charles Howard, Lord Howard of Effingham, later earl of Nottingham, lord chamberlain and lord high admiral; Sir John Popham, attorney general and chief justice of the King's Bench; and their many associates and subordinates—nearly 1,500 gentlemen and ladies of the court, many of them sons and daughters of the old families and peers of the realm or wards of the queen, waited in attendance to give homage to her and to be educated in the proper manners of the upper classes.

Naturally, in a restricted society like the court, cliques and hierarchies were constantly forming and re-forming. The queen was always the focus of the glittering splendor. Attendance on her presence was controlled not only by personal guards but also by special favorites who determined who would or would not be granted audience. At all times the queen demanded and received abject servility. Anyone in conference with her was required to kneel in her presence; even her most powerful ministers remained on their knees for hours if necessitated by the length of a session. In her absence, courtiers were required to bow or kneel three times while passing her empty seat in Whitehall Chapel. For those who pleased the queen, the rewards could be phenomenal. But Sir Robert Naunton, who knew Elizabeth's court well and served as master of the Court of Wards under the Stuarts, wrote that the queen's "rewards chiefly consisted in grants and leases of offices and places of judicature, but for ready money, and in great sums, she was very sparing." Nevertheless, such grants and leases were capable of producing wealth and would remain in force so long as the favor of the queen permitted; but they were subject to withdrawal at her pleasure. Thus, like the new sea-lanes, the court offered an avenue to wealth and fame, one probably more open during Elizabeth's reign than ever before or since.

There was another side to these enticing opportunities: the risk was equally great. Traffic on the newly opened oceans was hazardous, and mishaps of wind or weather or errors in judgment could wipe out the gains of many sound enterprises. Boarding a Spanish galleon might produce a fortune in gold or spices—or it might easily bring disablement or death. The favor of the monarch could raise one to undreamed-of affluence and authority; the disfavor was an unrestrained and could lead to torture, imprisonment, or death. The risks of the Elizabethan Age are graphically portrayed in the analysis of

Lord David Cecil, present-day descendant of the lords Cecil, Elizabeth's (and James's) most confidential advisers. According to Cecil, the

sixteenth century in England was a period of revolutionary change, during which a whole long-established political, religious, and economic system was overturned and a medieval country transformed into a modern one. Revolutionary change means chaos or the threat of it. To avoid this, people turned to strong government, in this case to virtual despotism of a new royal family, the brilliant and formidable family of Tudor, who ruled with the assistance of a new aristocracy, able and forcible as their masters, avid for wealth and power with little scruples as to how they got them. Indeed, the men and women who governed England during the first half of the sixteenth century, from the King downwards, had some of the characteristics of gangsters. And the world they lived in was, in many respects, a gangsters' world, violent, lawless, and unstable, the scene of a continuous struggle for domination fought by any means, however treacherous and brutal, and often literally to the death.

II. Ralegh the Elizabethan

It was into this turbulent society and court that Walter Ralegh came to play out his role as a natural leader and to become, in the minds of all later generations, a typical man of the Renaissance. As the times were violent, so his own life had only brief moments of calm; and he appears to have moved from extreme to extreme and to reflect the frenzied world depicted in one of the popular tragedies of Thomas Kyd or John Webster. As one of his contemporaries commented, "Sir Walter Ralegh was one that it seems fortune had picked out of purpose of whom to make an example, and to use as her tennis ball, thereby to show what she could do, for she tossed him up of nothing, and to and fro to greatness, and from thence down to little more than to that wherein she found him, a base Gentleman."

Actually, Ralegh came from an old and well-connected family in the west of England. His father, Walter Ralegh of Fardel, Devon, was a respected merchant who owned at least one ship for his trade and whose family had lived in the West Country for more than two centuries. The Walter Ralegh of this account was the second son of Katherine Champernoun, his father's third wife. (His father's first wife was Joan Drake, a cousin to the famous Sir Francis; to her were born two sons—George Ralegh, who inherited the Fardel estates, and John Ralegh. His second wife was the daughter of a Genoese merchant; to her was born a daughter, Mary.) From his mother, Walter Ralegh inherited an even more distinguished genealogy. As daughter of Sir Philip Champernoun of Modbury and his wife, Katherine Carew, Ralegh's mother claimed noble, if not regal, ancestry. As a rising courtier, Ralegh claimed more than usual gentility.

In 1586, when John Hooker, chamberlain of Exeter, wrote the history of Ireland for inclusion in Holinshed's famous *Chronicles,* he dedicated it to young Walter Ralegh, noting that "your ancestor Sir John de Ralegh married the daughter of deAmerie, Damerie of Clare, Clare of Edward the first, and which Clare by his father descended of King Henry the first. And in like manner by your mother you may

6

be derived of the same house." This may have been flattery, but in that same year, when Walter Ralegh applied for a genealogical review and the establishment of a coat of arms, he emphasized these connections.

More influential than these ancient ancestors in molding Ralegh's character, however, were contacts with members of the immediate family among whom he lived and worked. Katherine Champernoun's marriage to Walter Ralegh was her second marriage, and she brought children from both marriages into the new household. Her first husband was Otho Gilbert of Compton (from another old Devon family), and by him she bore three sons who achieved great fame. These were John Gilbert, Humphrey Gilbert (both of whom were knighted by Elizabeth), and Adrian Gilbert, all of whom took to sea to recoup the family fortunes. Though little is known of the life of Katherine Champernoun-Gilbert-Ralegh, it is obvious that she was the dominating force in her families inasmuch as her sons were endowed with strength of character not found in other members of their families. This family imprint on young Walter Ralegh is clearly pointed out by Professor A. L. Rowse in his recent study of Ralegh and his family:[1]

This mixed family of Gilberts and Raleghs had strong characteristics in common, evidently coming through the mother. John Gilbert and Carew Ralegh were mean and acquisitive, Humphrey Gilbert and Walter Ralegh acquisitive and extravagant. They all had a marked vein of intellectual interests, but (except for Adrian) they were men of action—that was what was interesting about them: with them ideas went to their heads, were liable to carry them away. They were speculators, projectors, bent not only on voyages across the seas, but voyages of the mind. Humphrey Gilbert was almost a *fantaisiste,* for ever cruising beyond the borders of the possible; and so he met his end. Adrian Gilbert was a dabbler in astrology, alchemy, necromancy. Walter Ralegh did not think as other men thought; with him an extremely sceptical intelligence went along with his soaring imagination. His heterodox opinions disregarded other men's; they rewarded him— and this was dangerous—by labelling him 'atheist.'

Passions stalked through this family. Sir Humphrey Gilbert was impetuous and rash to the verge of insanity. His brother John was perpetually involved in quarrels. Passion, rage, desperation were familiar companions with Ralegh. They were a dangerous lot. But they were gifted too: Adrian Gilbert at science; Carew Ralegh at music. . . . Walter Ralegh, as we know, had all the gifts of body and spirit, save happiness and peace of mind.

During the impressionable years of his teens and early manhood, young Walter Ralegh was subjected to the wide range of experience that Elizabethan life offered the young gentleman: at the age of fourteen he was sent to Oxford, to Oriel College, for the education expected of the gentry of his day. His records there are sparse, but it appears that he attended intermittently, coming and going between 1568 and 1571, though he took no degree. But at the same time he was learning the life of a scholar, he was learning the art of soldiering. He went to France to follow his relative, Henry Champernoun, who was raising a volunteer force of West Country men to aid the Huguenots in their battles against the Catholics. In his *Historie of the World,* written nearly a half century later, Ralegh indicated that he was present at the battle of Jarnac in March, 1569, and in the retreat

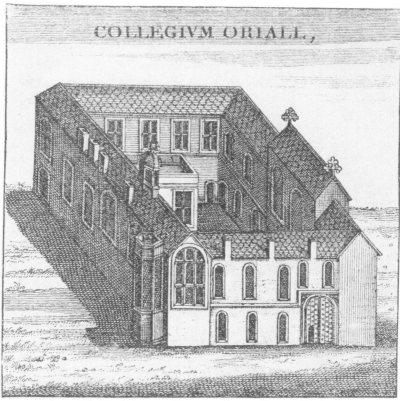

Walter Ralegh attended Oriel College, Oxford, intermittently from 1568 to 1571, although he took no degree. Engraving from Joseph Foster, *Alumni Oxoniensis: The Members of the University of Oxford, 1500-1714* (Oxford, England: Parker and Company, 4 volumes, 1891), II, facing p. 535.

of Moncontour the following October, periods during which he was still enrolled at Oxford.

Following this period as scholar and soldier, Ralegh moved at the age of twenty-three to London, center of the intellectual, social, and political life of England. There he was entered as a member of the Inner Temple, though he appears to have studied everything but law. (In later years he boasted that he never read law for a day in his life, but this probably was an exaggeration.) In London he grew familiar with the young poets of the time, particularly George Gascoigne, who may have turned Ralegh's eyes to the court by introducing him to Elizabeth's current favorite, the earl of Leicester. But young Ralegh did not settle down. As one of his contemporaries remarked, his "approaches to the University and Inns of Court were the grounds for his improvements, but they were rather excursions than sieges or settling down, for he stayed not long in a place." Although they were casually spent, these years did broaden the young Devonshire gentleman: they gave him insight into the abstract intellectual activities of the scholar and the brutal and painful life of the soldier— all this during his early twenties.

III. Ralegh Discovers the New World

It was through his family connections that young Walter Ralegh was first introduced to the new lands that were to dominate so many of his thoughts and ambitions for the rest of his life. His older half brother, Sir Humphrey Gilbert, was residing in London during Ralegh's early years there; and since they shared many mutual friends, they must have seen much of each other. A great deal of the talk of the city during the 1570s centered on the expanding horizons of the New World and of the role that England might play in the development of new lands. Such talk was natural to men reared in the West Country, where the sea was part of their daily lives and ambitions.

Sir Humphrey had lived as diverse a life as any young Elizabethan gentleman. Like his younger half brother, he had fought on the continent in the Protestant wars. After Eton he, too, had spent some time at Oxford, then had been attached to the household of Elizabeth and had become well known at court. During the years Ralegh was at the university, Gilbert was active in the English efforts to quell the Irish uprisings against England's attempts to establish colonies there. While thus engaged, he had risen from the ranks, had become colonel of Munster in 1569, and had been knighted the following year. In dealing with the Irish insurgents, Sir Humphrey was ruthless; he wrote to the lord deputy that he would hold neither peace nor parley with a rebel, that no conquered nation could be ruled with gentleness.

But even as he was subjugating the Irish lords by force, Gilbert's thoughts turned to the sea and to his ambitions to conquer new lands in America. As early as 1566 he had petitioned the queen to authorize him to seek a Northwest Passage to Cathay (China), but his application had gone unanswered. Nine years later he again raised the issue, but because of the objection of his elder brother, John, his request was denied and the patent given to Martin Frobisher. The following year Sir Humphrey sent the queen still another discourse, entitled "How Her Majesty might annoy the King of Spain by fitting out a fleet of warships under pretense of a voyage of discovery, and so fall upon the enemy's shipping, destroy his trade in Newfoundland and the West Indies, and possess both regions." Such a proposal un-

Sir Humphrey Gilbert, like his younger half brother, Walter Ralegh, was infatuated with the sea and with the possibilities of conquering new lands in America. Engraving from Alexander Brown, *Genesis of the United States* (Boston: Houghton, Mifflin, 2 volumes, 1890), I, facing p. 420.

doubtedly would have been attractive to young Walter Ralegh as well, since he shared both his brother's feelings about Spain and his desire to attack Spanish shipping on the high seas. Privateering, the sending of privately armed ships into battle to loot Spanish vessels, was a popular and profitable occupation during the continuing war with Spain, and ambitious Englishmen like Gilbert and Ralegh were attracted to it.

Such an occupation could not, of course, be approved openly by royal authority, so a great deal of negotiation to conceal the main purposes ensued. The outcome was that on June 11, 1578, letters patent were granted to Sir Humphrey Gilbert to conduct an expedition. The patent was somewhat vague concerning the specific destination of the expedition. Sir Humphrey was granted royal authority to "discover, search, find out, and view such remote heathen and barbarous lands, countries, and territories not actually possessed by any Christian prince or people as to him . . . shall seem good." Yet, even under this cover, Elizabeth protected herself: in the event any foreign prince should complain of hostility against his people or property, Gilbert was required to make restitution or he would be "put out of our allegiance and protection."

Under authority of this patent, Gilbert sent out a call to his brothers and relatives to obtain ships and to arm, supply, and man them for a voyage of exploration and possible colonization in the New World. On the surface, he was proposing to ally his exploration with his search for the anticipated Northwest Passage; underneath, he was almost without question planning a privateering venture. David B. Quinn, who has made the most complete study of Gilbert and his activities, points out that the timing of the expedition virtually ruled out an assault on the northern shores of America and, more significantly, that many of the captains enlisted for the venture were known pirates. In any case, this first major attempt at colonizing the New World was largely a family affair; and its failure was largely attributable to the rashness frequently exhibited by the sons of Katherine Champeroun-Gilbert-Ralegh.

Certainly, the aborted expedition of 1578-1579 cut deeply into the family fortunes inasmuch as the major costs were borne by Sir John, Sir Humphrey, and Adrian Gilbert and their half brothers, Walter and Carew Ralegh. Not many records of this voyage remain, but a short account, written by either John Stow or John Hooker, is in the 1587 edition of Holinshed's *Chronicles:*

. . . ten sails of all sorts of shipping, well and sufficiently furnished for such an enterprise, weighed anchor in the West Country and set to the sea. But God not favoring the attempt, the journey took no good success: for all the ships, enforced by some occasion or mischance, made their present return again; that only excepted wherein his brother Walter Ralegh was captain, who being desirous to do somewhat worthy honor, took his course for the West Indies, but for want of victuals and other necessaries (needful in so long a voyage) when he had sailed as far as the Islands of Cape de Verde upon the coast of Africa, was enforced to set sail and return for England. In this his voyage, he passed many dangerous adventures, as well by tempest as fights on the sea; but lastly he arrived safely at Plymouth in the West Country in May the next following.

Obviously, Ralegh's "dangerous adventures" were matters of piracy; and these "fights on the sea" by the inexperienced young Ralegh caused some consternation at court. When Sir Humphrey began preparations for a second expedition under his letters patent in the spring of 1579, the Privy Council sent orders "for revoking of him from his intended voyages at the seas for seeking of foreign countries." Sir Humphrey and Sir John replied that they had incurred no responsibilities for "spoils and injuries" and that to pull back at this late date would cause them considerable loss. Yet, the Gilberts' peaceable intents were thrown in doubt by the fact that while waiting for an answer, their men seized a Spanish ship at Dartmouth and confiscated its cargo of oranges and lemons. Again on May 28 the council addressed Sir John Gilbert, ordering him to restore the Spanish ship and to advise his brothers and Walter Ralegh "to surcease from

12

proceeding any further, to remain at home, and to answer such as have been by their companies damaged." At the same time, the council issued to the sheriff and justices of the peace orders to prevent any of the Gilberts' ships from putting to sea (by threatening "Her Majesty's indignation" toward any who left), to make special inquiries into the activities of Sir Humphrey and Walter and to imprison them if found guilty, to force their bonds for repayment, and to discharge their seamen.

Unfortunately, Ralegh's first sea experience, like those that were to follow, was thus not a happy or profitable one. It did, however, furnish him much experience and convince him that this was a life he loved, even though he found himself (as he was throughout life) a miserably poor sailor. The six months of this expedition also gave him, for the first time, the burdens of command. As captain of the *Falcon,* fourth largest of Sir Humphrey's fleet, Ralegh led a half dozen gentlemen adventurers and a complement of more than seventy sailors and soldiers. As commander, Ralegh was not called upon to navigate—that task lay to the pilot, Simon Fernandes, a Portuguese seaman who was to play a large role in Ralegh's later efforts at colonization. But it was Ralegh who maintained discipline among all on board, was responsible for all decisions affecting their activities, and, during battles, issued commands. These were competencies that Ralegh, then at the age of twenty-six, needed to master; they were to stand him in good stead for the remainder of his life.

IV. Back at Court

Disappointment over his failure to gain fame and fortune at sea embittered the young Walter Ralegh. Returning to London and finding himself still on the fringes of the court, he became sensitive and belligerent. Although records of the still relatively unknown young man are sparse, it is known that he was involved in at least two brawls during the early months of 1580. In February he quarreled with Sir Thomas Perrot, son of Sir John Perrot, who became president of Munster. What the argument was about is unknown (it probably had to do with the management of Irish affairs and proper treatment of Irish insurgents), but it was sufficiently severe to come to swordplay—and to the attention of the queen. The Privy Council, not taking sides in the matter, committed both men to Fleet Prison for six days to cool their blood. Even that did not work, for a month later, at the tennis court at Westminster, Ralegh became embroiled in another quarrel—with a man named Wingfield—and again the hot tempers of both men led them to cross swords. This time the Privy Council remanded Ralegh to Marshalsea Prison for a period of contemplation and remorse. Ralegh became known as a man of quick temper.

Eyewitness accounts of Ralegh during this period are at wide variance, depending upon what the viewer thought of the young man. English antiquary John Aubrey, who found humor in Ralegh's brawling disposition and his quick eye for a maid, noted that "He was a tall, handsome, and bold man; but his naeve was that he was damnably proud. . . . He had a most remarkable aspect, an exceeding high forehead, long-faced and sour eye-lidded, a kind of pig eye. His beard turned up naturally." Robert Naunton, author of an account of Queen Elizabeth's courtiers, knew Ralegh well; and although he was a close friend of Ralegh's rival, the earl of Essex, he was more generous:

He had in the outward man, a good presence, in a handsome and well compacted person, a strong natural wit, and a better judgement, with a bold and plausible tongue, whereby he could set out his parts to the best advantage; and to these he had the adjunct of some general learning, which, by diligence he enforced to a great augmentation and perfection, for he was an indefatigable reader, whether by Sea or Land, and none of the least observers both of men and of the times.

Ralegh's capacity for work and learning was stressed by many of his contemporaries. After Ralegh's death, David Lloyd wrote: "Five hours he slept, four he read, two he discoursed; allowing the rest to his business and his necessities." Extant portraits of the man show him to be well proportioned and handsome, as would be expected of one to be singled out by the queen, and ornately and richly dressed. Always he is seen wearing his badge of gentility, his sword, which he was willing and able to use for more than show. By nature, Ralegh was proud and vain, quick to take offense at any slight, real or imagined. He feared only poverty and the anger of his queen. He was able to capitalize on his rustic background: he took pride in his broad Devon accent and his country figures of speech, using them so effectively that they became a kind of trademark. And although he possessed an unusual lyric imagination, even for an Elizabethan, he spoke as he wrote—clearly, logically, forcefully, even bluntly—expressing his opinions and beliefs fearlessly in Parliament, in private conversations, and in conferences with the queen or her principal ministers. Ralegh was a strong and dynamic character; it was inevitable that he would create a stir in any society or situation in which he found himself.

V. Ralegh in Ireland

Ralegh badly needed to find some situation through which he could demonstrate his real abilities. Personality alone was not enough to do more than set him slightly above the mass of courtiers; and although he had become acquainted with Walsingham and won the notice of both Lord Burghley and Leicester, he was still undistinguished. It was the Irish wars that were to furnish him with the chance to use his qualities of courage and determination and to show his capacity for leadership.

During the 1570s and 1580s Ireland was a seething cauldron of revolt. The confiscation of monasteries that resulted from the break of the Church of England from the papacy came later in Ireland than it had in England proper, and, because of the strong pro-Catholic feelings of the people, raised more popular opposition. Attempts to quell local rioting were sporadically effective, but there was little or no real conversion to the new faith. Emotions were even more intensified when the pope commissioned James Fitzmaurice, a devout Munster nobleman, to liberate the island from the excommunicated English monarch and furnish mercenary soldiers to assist the natives in their revolts. Fitzmaurice was most effective in the south of Ireland, where he had more friends; and the province of Munster became the focus of the rebellion.

Munster was also the section of Ireland of most interest to the citizens of Devon and Cornwall, many of whom had large holdings there. Among those directly involved was the Gilbert family. Humphrey Gilbert had been interested in the Irish plantations of Munster since he soldiered there in the late 1560s, and his friends and relatives had joined him in acquiring property there. By the late 1570s the fate of Munster was important to all of them—the Gilberts, the Grenvilles, the Carews, the St. Legers, and their "cousins" the Zouches. Thus, it is easy to understand why, when in the summer of 1580 Baron Thomas Grey of Wilton was named lord deputy of Ireland and charged with putting down the insurrections from his headquarters in Dublin, Ralegh was given a commission as captain of a hundred foot soldiers and sent with Sir Warham St. Leger to augment the forces protecting English interests in the vicinity of Cork.

This was the opportunity Ralegh had been waiting for. Although his service in Ireland lasted only a year and a half, his unusual decisiveness and political acumen (perhaps aided by family connections) gave him the visibility he had wanted. Shortly after his arrival, Sir James of Desmond, one of the most feared rebels, was captured in battle, and Ralegh and Sir Warham St. Leger were commissioned to conduct his trial. They acted quickly and firmly. As John Hooker, sixteenth-century antiquary, reported, Desmond "was examined, indicted, arraigned, and then upon judgment drawn, hanged, and quartered, and his body being quartered, it was together with the head set on the town gate of the city of Cork." A bit later, when members of the Barry family were committing outrages (in English eyes), Ralegh rode to Dublin to ask Lord Grey for additional soldiers and permission to seek out the rebels in their own stronghold. On the way back, while leading his troops, Ralegh was caught in midstream by the Seneschal of Imokilly. To aid a fallen friend, Ralegh held off the entire force with his pistol until aid could arrive—an act heroic enough to impress even his Irish enemies. Later in the year, when Captain Zouch replaced the earl of Ormond as general of Munster, Ralegh was named as one of the commissioners governing that city. In this role Ralegh determined to bring Lord Roche, a popular Anglo-Irish chieftain, in for questioning, and with some trickery and a force of ninety men succeeded in doing so. In this dangerous mission only one life was lost.

By mid-1581 Ralegh had won the respect and confidence of all the Munster English. With Zouch he traveled widely among the people, attempting to stop revolts before they started. During these travels he gradually became dissatisfied with the English strategy. The mass of the peasants and many of the lesser nobles, he found, distrusted or hated the tyrannical overlords who were leading the rebellion. If given protection from these few leaders, he argued, they might rally to the support of the English government. The severe policies of Arthur, Baron Grey, lord-deputy of Ireland, Ralegh observed, worked against English success, since the more repressive the measures, the greater the reaction against them. Ralegh became convinced that it would be more expedient, more economical, and more humane for the English representatives to work with the Irish in solving their economic problems, to protect them from the oppressive "Hydra-heads," and to enlist their support and allegiance for a friendly queen who could foil the treasonable few who wanted to return Ireland to the pope.

This was a great change in policy position for Ralegh inasmuch as he had come to Ireland imbued with the stern principles of justice espoused by Sir Humphrey Gilbert and had, under orders, slaughtered soldiers, women, and children in the surrendered garrison of Smerwick. It was also in direct contradiction to the established beliefs of the puritan Lord Grey, under whom he held his commission. Grey was most unhappy with this critical assessment of his command, refused to pass on his reports, and rejected Ralegh's request for the grant of Barry's court for his own use. By the end of August, 1581, Ralegh was disillusioned and wanted to return to court in London. He wrote to Leicester: "I have spent some time here under the Deputy, in such poor place and charge as, were it not that I knew him to be one of yours, I would disdain it as much as to keep sheep." The antipathy was mutual. Grey wrote to Walsingham about Captain Ralegh: "For my own part, I must be plain: I neither like his carriage nor his company."

Finally, in December, 1581, Ralegh returned to London under a warrant, signed by Secretary Walsingham, "for bringing letters in post for her Majesty's affairs, from Cork in Ireland." Although Ralegh apparently did not give up his captain's commission (or his salary), his subsequent activities clearly demonstrate his belief that his services in Ireland had achieved their purpose and were at an end.

VI. Ralegh Gains Favor at Court

Following his return to London at the beginning of 1582, Ralegh lost no time in carrying his messages to Walsingham and was soon expressing his strong views about Ireland to him, to other principal officers, to the Privy Council, and to the queen herself. His presentations were forceful and made a strong impression. Aubrey, reporting on the gossips of the court, declared that Ralegh "told his tale so well, and with so good a grace and presence, that the Queen took especial notice of him and presently preferred him."

Sir Robert Naunton reported: "true it is, he [Ralegh] had gotten the Queen's ear in a trice, and she began to be taken with his election and loved to hear his reasons to her demands, and the truth is, she took him for a kind of Oracle." It was Ralegh's clear and reasoned analysis of a problem and his effective persuasion in an argument that appealed to the cautious Lord Burghley and his equally cautious and niggardly queen. Ralegh became almost an overnight wonder—an expert on the complex international affairs of the English-Irish-Catholic-Spanish controversy—and acquired a reputation as an acute political observer, a reputation that remained with him for the rest of his life. It was the quality of his mind as much as the attractiveness of his person that, in John Hooker's words, brought Ralegh "into the approved favor of your Prince who hath pleased to reward and honor in you the approved faithful service of your late ancestors and kindred deceased, and inclined her princely heart, conceiving a great hope of your own sufficiency and ability to restore you again."

Ralegh's rapid rise to favor, which caused much anger and opposition from those who felt they had been displaced, is evidenced not only by the grants, leases, and titles that were bestowed upon him by the queen but also from the fact that within a very short time he ceased his role as suitor to become a dispenser of favors—to come to the aid of even such eminent members of the court as Lord Burghley and the earl of Leicester. Correspondence among them shows Ralegh as frank and open, and it is apparent that his dealings with the queen were equally without guile. Yet, Ralegh's phrasings are deferential and conciliatory, without the harsh bluntness that could mark his

As a leading member of Elizabeth's court and increasingly a personal favorite of the Virgin Queen, Ralegh attracted a great deal of attention. This engraving of Ralegh in ultra-formal attire was rendered by H. Robinson after a painting by Zucchero in the collection of the Marquis of Bath. It was published in London by Harding and Lepard in 1836. Photograph from the files of the Division of Archives and History.

treatment of those of lesser importance; and they show Ralegh in his early thirties learning the manners of diplomacy.

In April, 1582, Ralegh's commission as captain of infantry for Ireland was renewed, but by the queen's express orders he was retained at court. The following year his improved estate became obvious: he was given a lease to Durham House, one of the most impressive and palatial residences in London, built on the banks of the Thames at the curve of the river, between Westminster and London Bridge. Before the Great Fire, Durham House was an impressive London sight.

In May Ralegh was granted two estates that had come to the queen as a gift from All Souls College, Oxford, and shortly thereafter she awarded him the grant of the "farm of wines"—the right to levy charges on every vintner who wished to sell wine. Ralegh leased the houses for ready cash and sublet the wine license for seven years at an annual rent that at the present time would approximate seventy thousand dollars. In May, 1584, an even greater reward came to him—a license to export woolen broadcloth, a major export commodity. This patent alone, energetically pursued as it was, brought Ralegh the equivalent of nearly a million dollars annually. Ralegh was rapidly acquiring the kind of wealth and power given to few men of his time.

VII. Ralegh's Thoughts Again Turn Westward

Ralegh, although he enjoyed his new life as the queen's plaything, was still most interested in enhancing his estate, position, and power. He envied his brother, Sir Humphrey Gilbert, for his patent to "search, find out, and view" the "barbarous lands" of the New World and to establish a base of operations for future English settlements there. Gilbert's patent was to expire in 1584, and, except for extensive planning and small exploratory expeditions under Simon Fernandes, nothing significant had been done since the aborted venture of 1579. But in early 1582 preparations for a larger voyage began in earnest. To finance it, Sir Humphrey offered grants of land in the New World to supporters and drew up elaborate plans concerning governance, implementation of public services, churches, and economic development in the regions yet to be established. Ralegh was enthusiastic about the potential of new English colonies; he not only bought shares in the company but also used some of his new wealth to build for the voyage an experimental ship of 200 tons, which he named the *Bark Ralegh* and hoped to command.

To prevent the catastrophic navigation that marked the first expedition, the famous John Dee, England's most noted mathematician and theoretical navigator, was enlisted to bring his skills to the planning. Richard Hakluyt, who had been teaching navigation and geography at Oxford, was also drafted to help (and a case could be made that his student at Oxford, Thomas Harriot, came with him, as did his "bedfellow in Oxford," Stephen Parmenius of Buda, who asked to make the voyage with Gilbert). Although it was Ralegh's intent to be second in command to Sir Humphrey, once more Elizabeth ruled that neither should go—Ralegh because she wanted him near her, and Gilbert because he was "a man noted of not good hap at sea." Ralegh protested, and his influence with the queen was such that she relented and gave her permission for Sir Humphrey to depart; Ralegh, however, was not allowed to join him.

On June 11, 1584, Gilbert's small fleet of five vessels sailed from Causand Bay, Devonshire. Carrying Sir Humphrey was the *Delight* (120 tons), the admiral of the fleet; the vice-admiral was the *Bark*

Ralegh, on which Ralegh had hoped to sail; the rear admiral was the 40-ton *Golden Hind* (not Drake's famous vessel). The fleet's two remaining ships were the *Swallow* (40 tons) and the *Squirrel* (10 tons). In spite of the apparent frenzy of activity in preparation, Gilbert's fleet was poorly outfitted. Food and supplies were totally inadequate for the long sea voyage. Not even the plans for the route were firm. At the last minute it was decided that the fleet, instead of following the normal sea-lanes that conformed to the prevailing winds, would instead sail a northern route to land in the vicinity of Newfoundland; this would enable the crews to augment their meager provisions with fish from the Grand Banks.

At midnight, two days after departing, the *Bark Ralegh* left the fleet to return to Plymouth because of sickness on board and lack of victuals. Gilbert was furious and asked Ralegh to discipline his crew. But from that point on, the voyage seems to have lost its focus. The vessels separated. The *Delight* and the *Golden Hind* left the others, sailing on alone to Newfoundland to meet with the Spanish, Portuguese, French, and English fishing vessels there. The *Swallow* robbed a ship to obtain provisions. The four ships made rendezvous again at St. John's, but the sailors of the *Delight* and the *Golden Hind* were so ill that they refused to go on. Sir Humphrey separated the sick from the well, left the *Swallow* to return the defectors to England, and continued on with the admiral, the rear admiral, and the tiny *Squirrel.* But there was still confusion as to their destination, and Gilbert's navigation had not improved. Soon afterward, the *Delight* ran aground and was wrecked. More than eighty men were drowned, all of Gilbert's maps and papers were lost, and the sixteen men who were spared the sea were assigned to the other ships. Only the *Golden Hind* and the *Squirrel* were left to carry the handful of survivors back to Plymouth. For some unknown reason, Gilbert insisted upon sailing with the tiny *Squirrel.*

Waters in the northern seas were rough and the passage was difficult, so the ships stayed in close contact. On Monday, September 9, as they sailed side by side, Hayes, captain of the *Golden Hind,* looked down from the higher desk of his vessel to see Sir Humphrey calmly reading a book. Hayes attempted to get Gilbert to come aboard the larger vessel, but Sir Humphrey refused. As Hayes later told the tale:

Monday the ninth of September, in the afternoon, the frigate was near cast away, oppressed by waves, yet at that time recovered: and giving forth signs of joy, the General [Gilbert], sitting abaft with a book in his hand, cried out unto us in the *Hind* (so oft as we did approach within hearing) We are as near to Heaven by sea, as by land. Reiterating the same speech, well beseeming a soldier resolute in Jesus Christ, as I can testify he was.

The same Monday night, about twelve of the clock, or not long after, [on] the frigate, being ahead of us in the *Golden Hind,* suddenly the lights were out, whereof as it were in a moment, we lost the sight, and withal our watch cried, the General was cast away, which was too true. For in that moment the frigate was devoured and swallowed up by the sea. Yet we still looked out all that night and ever after until we arrived upon the coast of England.

VIII. Ralegh Seizes the Initiative

The tragic loss at sea of his favorite brother in no way dampened Ralegh's enthusiasm for the potential of the New World as a source of fame and riches, and almost immediately he petitioned the queen for patents to acquire major portions of the new continent. His palatial new quarters in Durham House became the focus of much activity. William Sanderson, Ralegh's wealthy merchant in-law, was enlisting support of London traders; Sir Richard Grenville was soliciting ships and men in Ireland and in the West Country; Richard Hakluyt, who had gone to Paris as preacher for the British ambassador there, returned to London to prepare a document to interest the queen in the enterprise. And Ralegh's recent recruit from Oxford, Thomas Harriot, was given rooms in Durham House for use as a laboratory-library in gathering rutters,[2] maps, charts, and astronomical and navigational instruments and preparing for the instruction of Ralegh and his sea captains in the latest scientific techniques of deep-sea voyaging.

Ralegh's continuing supplications did not go unanswered. On March 14, 1584, at Westminster, Elizabeth put her hand above the privy seal on new letters patent to Walter Ralegh. This patent was almost identical, with only minor variations in wording, to the one granted six years earlier to Sir Humphrey Gilbert. But, as had been the case with Gilbert, Elizabeth was fearful that Ralegh might use his patent as a cover for piracy and that this might lead to open war with Spain. To forestall such a possibility, she detached the throne from any such illegal acts.

The patent gave Ralegh the opportunity for which he had been waiting, and he was now in a position in which with any luck he could render handsome service to both his queen and his country—and (of course) compound his personal fortune at the same time. Even the risk of loss of national protection did not deter him. Forces in the New World with which he might become engaged were those of the "foreign princes" of Spain and Portugal. And while England was not actively at war with these nations at this time, it could hardly be said that they were in perfect amity with Elizabeth. Knowing the queen as well as he did, Ralegh could be confident that if his ships returned to England with spoils from the gold fleets of those nations, Elizabeth's one-fifth share would assuage any horror she might express for the manner in which it was obtained and he would remain her darling.

IX. The 1584 Voyage of Discovery

Once his charter was in hand, Ralegh lost no time in getting action. Within a month he had a ship and a pinnace "furnished with all provisions" and ready to sail on an exploratory voyage to "discover that land which lies between Norembega [the entire east coast of America from Newfoundland southward, later called Virginia] and Florida in the West Indies." The flagship, undoubtedly the *Bark Royal*, was commanded by nineteen-year-old Philip Amadas, a young man of Ralegh's growing household; Simon Fernandes, who had already visited Virginia with Gilbert, was pilot. The pinnace was most likely Ralegh's *Dorothy,* commanded by Arthur Barlowe, who had been Ralegh's lieutenant in the Irish wars. Nothing is known of other passengers, since the only report of this voyage is the short account given by Barlowe to Ralegh and printed by Hakluyt without elaboration. A propaganda publication, this account is, as David Quinn notes, "studiously vague" as to details, omitting known difficulties and provocative in what it omits. Besides the two captains and the pilot, only seven members of the company are named; and their roles are not identified. It can be surmised from Ralegh's way of operating that there must have been specialists for gathering information on which to base later voyages. By his own later count of ocean crossings, John White, who was to figure so large in subsequent colonial efforts, must have been aboard—probably to draw maps, sites, and people. And, Quinn argues, it is highly probable that White's companion, Thomas Harriot, also was on board, charged with "dealing with the natural inhabitants," as he was to do later. Although one can only speculate, this preliminary voyage must have added a great deal of sound information for later planning.

While his friends and servants were gathering information in the New World, Ralegh began to prepare for a more permanent settlement. This, he recognized, called for greater resources than he personally could give; to be fully effective, it should have the authority, support, and resources of the crown. Although he was aware that his personal influence on Elizabeth was great, Ralegh also knew her conservative nature and her unwillingness to assume obligations. To forestall her anticipated objections, Hakluyt prepared a propaganda document. Although it was not published until the nineteenth century, this document, generally referred to as *A Discourse of Western Planting,* emphasized the value of the New World as a source of commodities that were unavailable in England. But Hakluyt's (and Ralegh's) arguments went far beyond this aspect of the New World. They stressed the moral imperative that the queen, as head of the Church of England and "Defender of the Faith," must act to expand the boundaries of true Christianity. It was also asserted that these efforts on behalf of colonization would not only increase English commercial wealth but would also revitalize English trade, employ idle workers, and bring to the English citizen the riches of the Indies, Asia, and Africa. (But the document's final chapters reveal Ralegh's aspirations to use the charter to undermine the activities of Spain in the New World and to make England the preeminent nation.)

As presented to the queen, the *Discourse* concluded with a chapter recapitulating all of Ralegh's arguments. In reading Hakluyt's words, one can almost hear the eloquent Ralegh enunciating them in his broad Devon accent:

> This enterprise may stay the Spanish King from flowing all over the face of . . . America, if we seat and plant there in time. . . . Her Majesty may, by the benefit of the seat, having won good and royal havens, have plenty of excellent trees for masts, of goodly timber to build ships and make great navies, of pitch, tar, hemp, and all things incident for a royal navy, and that for no price and without money or request.

In mid-September, shortly after Hakluyt finished his appeal, Ralegh's two ships arrived safely in the West of England, Amadas and Barlowe having spent six weeks exploring the mid-Atlantic coastline. Although they brought no gold or silver, they did return with treasures of value as propaganda: Indian artifacts and two Indian "Princes"—Manteo and Wanchese— in full native attire. The stolid, quiet dignity of these two young men was most impressive to the more emotional English. They entranced the queen and were taken into the circles of the court, where during the autumn of 1584 they became social lions in London. Gradually they began to learn English, to the delight of their hosts, and America, long a popular subject of conversation, enjoyed an even greater vogue.

Barlowe's report of the expedition, clearly a skillful propaganda document, was widely circulated by Ralegh to appeal to the cupidity of investors or the adventurousness of future settlers. Barlowe and his fellow sailors could bear testimony to the warmth and friendliness of Ralegh's Virginia. Their two barks, he reported, had crossed the trade routes used by the Spanish, and they had first seen the American coast in the southern area that the Spanish held. There they "found the air very unwholesome, and our men grew for the most part ill disposed," so they replenished supplies and hurried on. But shortly thereafter, on July 2, they had arrived at the thirty-sixth parallel of latitude, where Ralegh proposed to establish his English foothold; and there "we found shoal water, which smelled so sweetly and was so strong a smell as if we had been in the midst of some delicate garden, abounding with all kinds of odiferous flowers." Having landed on a sandy island, they found no barrenness; rather, it was "so full of grapes as the very beating and surge of the sea overflowed them, of which we found such plenty . . . that I think in all the world the like abundance is not to be found: and myself having seen those parts of Europe that most abound, find such differences as were incredible to be written." The superlatives continued:

This Island had many goodly woods, full of Deere, Conies, Hares, and Fowle, even in the midst of Summer, in incredible abundance. The woodes are not such as you finde in Bohemia, Muscovia, or Hyrcania, barren and fruitlesse, but the highest, and reddest Cedars of the world, farre bettering the Cedars of the Azores, of the Indias, or of Lybanus, Pines, Cypress, Sassafras, the Lentisk or the tree that beareth the Mastic, the tree that beareth the rinde of black cinnamon . . . and many others of excellent smell, and qualitie.

Like the land, the natives were hospitable, "most gentle, loving, and faithful, void of all guile and treason, and such as lived in the golden age." Truly, Barlowe reported, Ralegh's Virginia seemed in all ways to reflect the idyllic Garden of Eden before the fall of Adam.

The earth brings forth all things in abundance, as in the first creation, without toil or labor. The people only care to defend themselves from the cold, in their short winter, and to feed themselves with such meat as the soil affords; their meat is very well sodden, and they make broth very sweet and savory; their vessels are earthen pots, very large, white, and sweet; their dishes are wooden platters of sweet timber; within the place where they feed was their lodging, and within that their Idol, which they worship, of which they speak incredible things.

Best of all, Barlowe reported, an ideal site for an English colony had been discovered—an interior island protected from possible Spanish invaders and located near friendly natives whose behavior could be judged by that of Manteo and Wanchese. Barlowe poetically described Roanoke Island in his narrative:

. . . in this enclosed sea there are about a hundred islands of divers bigness, whereof one is sixteen miles long, at which we were, finding it to be a most pleasant and fertile ground, replenished with goodly cedars and divers other sweet woods, full of currants, of flax, and many other notable commodities, which we at that time had no leisure to view.

Obviously, the Elizabethan public, although enraptured with such travel accounts, was skeptical about their truthfulness. Convincingly written though Barlowe's work seemed, there was no mad rush to sail to this island paradise—Ralegh's Eden, as it was later to be called. Yet Ralegh and his friends still held firm their belief in the high destiny of the land named for their queen.

X. Preparation for the 1585 Colonial Venture

Ralegh wanted more than the approval of the queen: he wanted his settling of Virginia to be a national enterprise and to have the financial support of the nation as well as of the adventurers. In 1584, among his other honors, he had been elected to Parliament as a representative of Devon. Although it was not necessary or even conventional, he decided to have his royal patent formally approved by legislative as well as executive authority. In December he introduced in both houses a bill to confirm his rights of exploration and settlement. Between December 13 and 18, 1584, this bill was read in the House of Commons and passed. But there, for some reason, the matter rested; and consideration in the House of Lords was halted. It may have been the queen who decided that parliamentary confirmation of royal grants was bad policy; or the lords may have felt that they had no authority in such matters. But no pique existed, for on the twelfth night, January 6, 1585, Elizabeth laid the blade of her royal sword on Ralegh's shoulder and named him Sir Walter, Lord and Governor of Virginia. In so doing, she honored not only the man but also the land, inasmuch as she named it in her honor as the Virgin Queen to replace the awkward Indian name of Wingandacoa, which it had previously borne, and gave tacit approval to Ralegh's dreams of extending her empire into the wilderness of America.

Without question, Ralegh's great ambition was to head the next expedition himself. Since his abortive voyage with Sir Humphrey Gilbert six years earlier, Ralegh had dreamed of establishing himself as a naval hero. But he had learned from bitter experience and from the example of his brother that the course of the sea was fraught with peril and that seamanship involved more than desire or effort—it required knowledge and skill of a high order. So in addition to seeking men, ships, and supplies, he set about acquiring the necessary skills for himself and in those sea captains who would serve under him. Perhaps on the advice of Hakluyt or Dee, he selected Thomas Harriot, one of the most promising young scientists and mathematicians of the day, from his alma mater, Oxford, to join him in his venture.

Recent discoveries of the papers of Thomas Harriot provide some

To accompany and assist him during his voyage of 1585, Ralegh selected Thomas Harriot, a promising young scientist and mathematician. Harriot's work was invaluable in preparing the members of the 1585 expedition for their tasks. Engraving of Harriot by Francis Delaram, 1620; reproduced by courtesy of the trustees of the British Museum, London.

insight into the navigational instruction that Ralegh and his captains were taking in preparation for their Virginia voyages. The papers reveal that Harriot, on the roof of Durham House, built a *radius astronomicus* 12 feet in diameter, with which to take astronomical observations more accurate than any previously taken in England. There he conducted classes, using as a text a manuscript book he had prepared and named *Arcticon* for the pole or guiding star. In this volume he discussed the navigational instruments of the time—the cross staff, the astrolabe, the sea ring, the compass, and the lead and line—and demonstrated how to use them most accurately and how to avoid common errors. There is some evidence that Harriot over-saw for Ralegh and each of Ralegh's captains the manufacture of special instruments of a size and weight that each was comfortable with and corrected them to accommodate the shapes of their respective faces. He even experimented with a back staff, which used the shadow of the sun at noon for taking latitude readings, instead of the conventional staff, which utilized the edge of the sun. The captains were taught how to determine exact latitude from the north star at night or from the sun at noon. Instruction was quite sophisticated.

31

Calculations were made to correct for the distance between the pupil of the eye and the base of the staff, for the height of the eye plus the height of the deck above the waterline, and for the variation of the position of the north star from true north. Each lesson ended with problems requiring precise mathematical solutions of the type that would be required at each stage of the journey. Harriot made tables showing the amount of correction required for each degree of latitude traversed, gave interpolations, and furnished methods of "proving" the answers. Without question, Ralegh's seamen were the best that experience and training could furnish him.

It was in February, while with the court at Somerset House, that Ralegh learned that the queen was again reluctant for him to leave the country and that he would be denied the pleasure of leading the first colony himself. Last-minute changes in leadership had to be made: the role Ralegh had hoped to fill was split. Sir Richard Grenville, of an old Cornish family, who had not previously been associated with Ralegh but who had been a member of Parliament and of the committee that confirmed Ralegh's patent and a subscriber to the venture, was placed in charge of the sea crossing and given the dual titles of general and admiral during the period of exploration. Ralph Lane, one of the queen's equerries and a soldier with more than a decade of experience as a privateer, was to be governor of the colony once it was established on land. Obviously, the queen had a hand in the selection of these leaders; and to assuage Ralegh's disappointment at being left behind, she contributed one of her ships, the *Tiger*, as flagship for the voyage and possibly some money for supplies. Sir Francis Walsingham also was a contributor, as were Grenville and the rich merchant William Sanderson.

As his own personal representatives in the party, Ralegh selected two trusted friends and associates; they were to be his eyes and ears and (to some extent) his authority in the exploration, discovery, and repoorting that was to follow. John White, a keen observer and a skilled artist, was to make maps, charts, and rutters and to draw pictures of the flora, fauna, and inhabitants of Virginia. Harriot was to assess the resources of the new land, both for the support of the colonists and for commerce, and was, in his own words, "in dealing with the natural inhabitants specially employed."

Harriot had prepared himself as meticulously as he had prepared the captains. During the ocean crossing he took nautical observations, checked compass variations, and recorded winds and water currents. On April 19, ten days out of Plymouth, he made observations of an

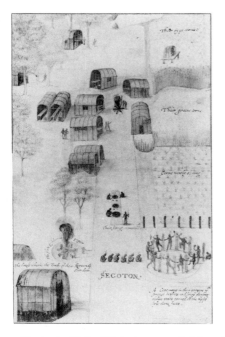

Typical of John White's masterful drawings rendered during the voyage of 1585 are these watercolors of the Indian village of Secotan *(left)* and an Indian in body paint. From *America 1585: The Complete Drawings of John White,* edited by Paul Hulton. Published by the University of North Carolina Press. Copyright 1984. Used with permission of the publisher.

eclipse of the sun, and at each landfall he collected specimens—fruits and vegetables, sugar, tobacco, ginger, and pearls—as evidence for future trade, while White made drawings as part of his record. Harriot also took with him instruments for use in Virginia in obtaining what probably were the first scientific readings in America. As he later reported, these impressed the Indians:

Most things they saw with us, as mathematical instruments, sea compasses, the virtue of the loadstone in drawing iron, a perspective glass whereby were showed many strange sights, burning glasses, wild-fire works, guns, books, writing and reading, spring clocks that seem to go of themselves, and many other things that we had, were so strange unto them and so far exceeded their capacities to comprehend the reason and means how they should be made and done, that they thought were rather the works of gods than of men, or at the leastwise they had been given and taught us of the gods.

Even more impressive was Harriot's preparation for his study of the natives. He recognized, as most early voyagers failed to do, that

33

to understand Indian culture required that he be able to communicate with the natives and not merely observe them. Carolinian Algonquian being a difficult language, Harriot must have devoted considerable time to learning it. Certainly, he spent long hours in close companionship with Manteo and Wanchese—if not during the first voyage, then during their return with Grenville and Lane. In all likelihood it was he who taught Manteo and Wanchese English during the winter of 1584-1585, as they taught him their own language. But Harriot went beyond this. To transcribe the sound of the original language, and knowing that the standard alphabet was not adequate for that complex task, Harriot, as his manuscripts reveal, studied the physical process of sound production and constructed for the first time a sophisticated phonetic alphabet—unique for its time and modern in its approach—to use in recording the natives' names and expressions in a way that would permit their accurate reproduction at any time. Difficult though it was, Harriot was so successful that when he reached the New World he could converse with the native tribesmen in their own language with some fluency. In his *Briefe and True Report of the New Found Land of Virginia* (1588), he says that he learned "the sum of their religion . . . by having special familiarity with some of their priests" and that the natives "through conversing with us . . . were brought into great doubts of their own [religion]."

Harriot, in addition to talking with the Indians, wished to compile a glossary of names and phrases. For his published *Report* he transcribed them back into the standard alphabet—his symbols would have been meaningless to the lay reader—using "Pagatowr" for maize, "Wickonzowr" for wild peas, "Macocqwer" for "Pompions, Mellons, and Gourds," and "Vppowoc" for tobacco. All in all, Harriot's *Report* contains thirty-three Indian names of native products, not counting place names and personal names. But from his own observations, these represent but a small part of the vocabulary he recorded during his year with the Indians. For example, he notes:

I have the names of eight and twenty several sorts of beasts which I have heard of to be here and there dispersed in the country, especially in the mainland: of which there are only twelve kinds that we have discovered. . . . Of all sorts of fowls I have the names in the country language of fourscore and six. . . . There are many other strange trees whose names I know not but in the "Virginian" language.

Harriot's dictionary, certainly a novelty, must have been circulated among those interested in Virginia and in additional voyages, but, like many other such manuscripts, it has disappeared and has never been recovered. Although there exists some evidence that it survived until the late seventeenth century, no such documents remain among Harriot's papers at the present time.

Advance planning for the voyage suffered, however, because the purpose of the proposed colony was not completely clear. Hakluyt, for instance, wanted the colony to be a permanent, self-supporting settlement modeled on the English town. An appendage to his *Discourse of Western Planting* was "A note of some things to be prepared for the voyage," which clearly shows this design. Not to be forgotten were the seeds, plants, fowls, and animals needed to start the colony; the foods and spices to tide the colonists over till the first crops were harvested; the artisans to build houses and make clothes; and the butchers, barbers, shoemakers, and bottle makers necessary to serve the colony. Another plan was offered by a soldier friend of Ralegh. In the Essex County Record Office in a manuscript endorsed "For Master Ralegh's Voyage." It proposed a strong military colony with at least 800 soldiers to protect the colony from Indians and marauding Spaniards. A hundred sentinels were to be on duty night and day, and security of fortifications was given high priority. The colony was to be run like a military camp, with an admiral leading the sea forces, a general the land, and a high treasurer to guard the gold and silver expected to be found and to protect the interests of the queen. Beneath such disparate plans Ralegh's dreams of empire could well be lost, and at least some of the difficulties of the first colony, as will be seen, were a result of uncertainty as to what its primary functions were to be.

XI. The First Virginia Colony, 1585-1586

The flotilla that sailed from Plymouth on April 9, 1585, was a modest one. Plymouth shipping records indicate that only "vi ships and barks" carrying "vi hundred men or thereabouts" constituted this first attempt to gain an English foothold on the upper east coast of America. Leading the fleet was the queen's *Tiger,* a galleass listed variously as 140 or 200 tons, which carried the leaders of the expedition. In addition to Sir Richard Grenville, who acted both as admiral and general at sea, and Governor Ralph Lane, who was in command while on land, were Simon Fernandes, pilot of the fleet, and most of the gentlemen of the council—Thomas Harriot and John White; Grenville's half brother, John Arundell; his brother-in-law, John Stukeley; and other gentlemen of the West Country, a Kendall and a Prideaux. Of the 160 men aboard, about half were soldiers and the remainder gentlemen or sailors. Two of Ralegh's own ships followed: the 140-ton flyboat *Roebuck,* under command of Captain John Clark, and the 100-ton *Lion* or *Red Lion,* commanded by George Raymond. Following these were the 100-ton *Elizabeth,* commanded by Thomas Cavendish and probably owned by him, and the 50-ton *Dorothy,* possibly commanded by Arthur Barlowe. Two pinnaces, valuable for sailing in shallow waters, were towed behind the *Tiger* and either the *Lion* or the *Roebuck.* The manpower totaled about 600: about a third were soldiers, armed for protection against natives or Spaniards; half were sailors, destined to stay with the ships on their return; and the remaining hundred were men recruited (on the promise of a grant of land) to stay through at least a year in Virginia.

Much too little is known of these recruits to assess their potential for building a sound settlement; nor can it be told how carefully they were chosen. Hakluyt printed the names "of all those as well Gentlemen as others that remained one whole year in Virginia under the government of Master Ralph Lane"—107 in all. Of these, fourteen were called "Master," indicating their status as gentlemen; one was a "Captain" (there was another captain among the gentlemen); and three, possibly servant boys, were listed by their first names only—Daniel, Smolkin, and Robert. For the remainder, identification is difficult: the names are common English ones found throughout England in various spellings. Although both David B. Quinn and William S. Powell have spent much time searching extant records for clues as to the identities of these men, identifications are in most cases conjectural. All that can be said with certainty is that they represent a cross section of Elizabethan society: younger sons of gentle families seeking adventure; recent graduates from the university attracted by the novelty of living among the gentle savages; servants following their masters into the wilds; a few specialists like Harriot and White and the master metallurgist Doughan Gannes (or, more accurately, Joachim Ganz); and a fairly large number of the lower element of English society, conscripted from the dives and taverns or released from prison as forced labor for the project.

One of Hakluyt's arguments in favor of the settlement of Virginia was that such a colony would provide fruitful employment to idle and unproductive prisoners. Ralegh's patent from the queen authorized him to recruit from prisons, and it seems likely that he did so. When he took his patent to the House of Commons for ratification, there was much discussion of the almost unlimited conscription authority he had been granted, and an amendment was proposed to deny him any authority over "any person or persons being in prison, either upon execution at the suit of any person for debts or being imprisoned or under arrest for any other cause whatsoever." But with the failure of Parliament to act, the original provisions stood and Ralegh had almost total freedom to fill vacancies in his ranks with anyone available, from prison or not.

It is unfortunate for Virginia and for history that this first English colony did not live up to the high dreams of Sir Walter, Hakluyt, Harriot, and White. From lack of clear purpose, from haste in recruitment of personnel, and from lack of understanding of the psychological demands placed upon a settler in a totally alien environment, the venture was doomed from the start. From this distance, it is easy to see the mistakes they made; but Ralegh and his trusted leaders were too close to their violent battles in Ireland, to the hatred that marked their contacts with the Spaniards and the Portuguese, to see what was needed to sustain a viable settlement in the wilderness of Virginia. Although there were a few dissenting voices in council, the decisions of Grenville and Lane were based on military considerations, and the colony was a military camp. Discipline was rigid; major activities were marching, fighting, or sentry duty. Construction was for fortification, protection of materiel, or housing for the superiors of the council. Little thought was given to the elements of husbandry (in all its many meanings) extolled by Hakluyt in his planning; much was given to exploitation of the land and its peoples, and when gold and pearls were not easily had, the majority of the settlers, like unemployed soldiers of that day, sat and complained instead of working to improve their lot for the future. Such attitudes were repulsive to many, ill feelings broke out, and discipline and organization deteriorated instead of improving with experience. The tale of the colony, told by both Lane and Harriot, is too well known to repeat here, but it came as a shock to Sir Walter and forced him to the realization that even greater efforts were needed if his high hopes for England were to be realized. Follow-up action had to be immediate.

The attitude of disgruntlement that permeated the colony in its last months filtered back to England from the returning fleet and made Ralegh's preparation for subsequent colonies more difficult than it otherwise would have been. And the following summer, with Sir Francis Drake's arrival in England from the New World (a hasty and ill-planned retreat occasioned by the failure of Lane's men to live frugally and in harmony with the Indians), the smoldering discontent broke out in open antagonism to the notion of further exploration and settlement in the New World. To check these vicious attacks, Ralegh asked Harriot to recapture in his *Briefe and True Report* some of the glamour and potential of life in Virginia. To counter the unfavorable reports, therefore, Harriot attacked the attackers; their evil reports, he insisted, could not be taken seriously because they, in their shallowness, had been responsible for the failure. Harriot wrote that

The cause of their ignorance was, in that they were . . . never out of the Island where we were seated [Roanoke], or not far, or in the leastwise in few places else, during the time of our [being] in the country; or of that many that after gold and silver was not so soon found, as it was by them looked for, had little or no care of any other thing but to pamper their bellies; or of that many which had little understanding, less discretion, and more tongue than was needful or requisite.
Some also were of a nice bringing up, only in cities or towns, or such as never (as I may say) had seen the world before. Because there were not to be found any English cities, nor such fair houses, nor at their own wish any of their old accustomed dainty food, nor any soft beds of down or feathers; the country was to them miserable, & their reports thereof according.

Although Harriot's denigrations may be overdrawn to discredit the harsh criticisms of the colonial experience by some of the colonists, there was obviously some basis for his report. Ralegh was to learn that many of those who involved themselves in the exploration of the New World did so only from selfish, short-term ambitions. Few shared with Sir Walter his idealistic dream of using the western continent for dual purposes: to build the resources of England as an emerging world power and to weaken and curtail the extent of empire and the aspirations of their Spanish rivals.

XII. Meanwhile, Back in England

Things were not going well back in London either. These were perilous years for England, and the queen, her ministers, and her court followers were all involved in plots and machinations of various sorts. The enmity with Spain that had festered for so many years was coming to a head. Although both Elizabeth and King Philip of Spain had clung tenaciously to hopes for peace, it was now obvious that their aspirations were infringing on each other. Spain's annexation of Portugal in 1580 had united two huge navies and made Spain dominant on the seas. In response, English privateering had mushroomed and, although merely irritating at first, had now seriously begun to interfere with Spain's exploitation of the new lands to the west. The excommunication of Elizabeth by the Catholic church added fuel to the hatred and focused world attention on Spain as the center of Catholicism and England as the seat of Protestantism. By the time Ralegh was sending Grenville and Lane on their first serious colonial effort, Philip was concluding that war between the two nations was inevitable.

Naturally Ralegh, like other members of the anti-Spanish faction, was not averse to accepting the challenge. Even while planning settlements near the thirty-sixth parallel of latitude in what became North Carolina, he was also preparing for further piracy against the Spanish plate fleet. He joined with the huge military and naval expeditionary venture being raised by England's hero, Sir Francis Drake, and the son-in-law of Walsingham, Christopher Carleill. But as was often the case, King Philip moved first. He ordered the confiscation of all English ships in Spanish ports and imprisoned their crews. According to popular legend, only one "tall ship of London" escaped his nets to bring back to England a captured letter that betrayed his plans for an invasion of Britain.

These were overt acts of war, and Elizabeth quickly abandoned her pose of neutrality to recognize officially the sea warfare that had been going on for several years. Drake's new venture was given authority to strike at the West Indies, to lead a fleet of more than twenty-five ships and pinnaces carrying nearly 2,300 soldiers, and to capture a base in the area of Spanish influence—most likely Cartagena. The war with Spain was well under way.

Early in October, 1585, Master John Arundell of Tolverne, who had sailed from Roanoke on August 5 in one of the fastest captured vessels, arrived at the court at Richmond bearing letters from Governor Lane to the queen, Walsingham, Sir Philip Sidney, and other supporters of Ralegh's colony. Lane asked for new supplies to replace those lost at landing and more armaments for the defense of the fort, which was being established as a winter base. But he also brought glowing accounts of the wealth and beauty of the new land, the friendliness of the natives, and the high morale of the settlers. In his letter to Walsingham, Lane sent the good news that

by the universal opinion both of our apothecaries and all our merchants here, of this Her Majesty's new kingdom of Virginia, all the kingdoms and states of Christendom, their commodities joined in one together, do not yield either more good or more plentiful . . . for public use . . . or pleasing for delight.

To Richard Hakluyt the elder he was more specific:

we have discovered the main[land] to be the goodliest soil under the cope of heaven, so abounding with sweet trees that bring such sundry rich and most pleasant gums, grapes of such greatness, yet wild, as France, Spain, nor Italy hath no greater, so many sorts of apothecary drugs, such several kinds of flax and one kind like silk, the same gathered of a grass as common there as grass is here. And now within these few days we have found here a Guinea wheat whose ear yields corn for bread, 400 on an ear, and the cane makes a very good sugar. . . . Besides that, it is the goodliest and most pleasing territory of the world (for the soil is of a huge, unknown greatness, and very well peopled and towned, though savagely), and the climate so wholesome that we have had not one sick since we touched land here. . . .

Obviously, these reports pleased Ralegh, the queen, and the well-wishers of the new colony. On October 14 the queen showed her gratitude by knighting John Arundell.

Ralegh was in Plymouth on October 18 when Sir Richard Grenville arrived with fresh news of the Roanoke colonists. Grenville's fleet had left Virginia twenty days after Arundell, but the delay was a blessing in disguise for Ralegh and the adventurers. Off Bermuda, Sir Richard in the *Tiger* had met up with the flagship of the Spanish Santo Domingo squadron and after a brief battle had captured what proved to be a rich prize indeed. According to Spanish invoices, the ship, the *Santa Maria* of San Vincente, carried more than 40,000 ducats in gold, silver, and pearls. Its cargo also included more than 100 tons of sugar, 50 tons of ginger, and 7,000 hides, together worth another 80,000 ducats. After taking the vessel, Grenville transferred a hundred of its seamen to the *Tiger* for ransom and boarded the *Santa Maria* to sail it to London.

How this wealth was distributed is still not clear. Grenville insisted there were no pearls or precious metals aboard; and for the cargo he estimated a mere 40,000 or 50,000 ducats. Approximately 15,000 pounds were distributed to investors, which David Quinn estimates gave them about a 50 percent profit for the entire expenditure. But there is some evidence that Grenville (and probably Ralegh) received more than this. Later court investigations indicate that there were elephant tusks aboard and that Grenville had kept two and had given five to Adrian Gilbert, four to Sir Walter, and two to Carew Ralegh. In a biography of Sir Walter published in 1959, Professor Willard Wallace estimated that the capture of the *Santa Maria* alone "enabled Ralegh to pay off his investors, to replenish his own depleted funds, and to purchase supplies and equip a ship to send out to Lane" for relief.

During the winter of 1585-1586 Ralegh could have had no premonition that Lane and his colonists would hurriedly leave their foothold in Virginia after residing there slightly less than a year and before their supplies and reinforcements arrived. He had expected some adjustments—that some colonists who found the rigors of the new land more than they could bear would be replaced and that additional supplies would be needed. But he certainly anticipated more positive results from this first attempt than he received. He expected to have a secure harborage for large ships that could serve as a base for supplying and refurbishing English vessels on marauding expeditions against the Spanish. He hoped to have a well-established community, largely self-supporting, with flourishing flocks, herds, and crops to sustain them and any new recruits who might follow. He had full confidence that the colony would have the willing support of the Indian tribes, as Manteo and Wanchese had promised. It was on these premises that Ralegh and Grenville worked to prepare relief for the following year.

Unfortunately, reality did not live up to expectations, as frantic and hurried decisions made under stress ended such early hopes. Hakluyt tells the story vividly in his 1589 *Principall Navigations.* According to this account, Raleigh had strained his credit to prepare a 100-ton vessel "freighted with all manner of things in most plentiful manner for the supply and relief of his colony." But the relief expedition started out late—after Easter. In the meantime, the Roanoke settlers, fearful that support was not coming, bravely prepared for an extended stay, planting large plots for supplies more than adequate to maintain them through another year. On the tenth of June, Sir Francis Drake, who had been raiding the Spanish on Santa Domingo, Cartagena, and Saint Augustine, decided to visit the English colony. He anchored his vessels off the Outer Banks and proceeded to Roanoke to confer with the leaders of the expedition to see how they fared and if the Spanish had bothered them.

Although the colonists reported that all was well, they nevertheless recalled the hardships of the previous winter and suggested that Drake, from his large flotilla, "leave with them three ships, that in some reasonable time they heard not out of England they might then return themselves." To this Drake agreed, and he also pressed on the colonists additional supplies that would keep them in fair comfort for the coming year.

But fickle nature interfered with these plans. As the colonists were busy relating their experiences and hardships to their visitors and preparing letters for them to take back to England, "a great storm arose and drove the most of [Drake's] fleet from their anchors to sea, in which ships at that instant were the chiefest of the English colony." This departure of the fleet panicked the settlers remaining on land, who,

Sir Francis Drake visited the English colony at Roanoke in June, 1586, and agreed to equip it with three ships and additional supplies. When a "great storm" arose, driving most of Drake's fleet out to sea, the colonists, temporarily panicked, persuaded Drake to convey them back to England. Engraving from copy in North Carolina Collection.

perceiving this, hasted to those three sails which were appointed to be left there, and for fear they should be left behind, left all things so confusedly as if they had been chased from thence by a mighty army, and [Hakluyt moralizes] no doubt so they were, for the hand of God came upon them for the cruelty and outrages committed by some of them against the native inhabitants of that Country.

According to Hakluyt, Ralegh's supply ship arrived almost immediately after the departure of the colonists. Searching briefly for the settlers and not finding them, Ralegh's captain became discouraged, and the ship returned to England with all its supplies. Just fourteen or fifteen days after that, Sir Richard Grenville, still considering himself to be governor of Virginia, arrived with

three ships which he had provisioned for the supply of the colonists: who, not finding the aforesaid ship according to his expectations, nor hearing any news of the English colony there seated and left by him, Anno 1585, himself travel[ed] up into divers places of the Country, . . . to see if he could hear any news of the Colony . . . but after some time spent therein not finding any news of them and finding the place which they inhabited desolate, yet unwilling to lose the possession of the country which Englishmen had so long held . . . , he determined to leave some men behind to retain possession of the country: whereupon he landed 15 men on the Isle of Roanoke, furnished plentifully with all manner of provision for two years, and so departed for England.

Hakluyt makes these actions appear plausible; other evidence raises doubts. Why, for example, did the master of Ralegh's supply ship, finding no one at Roanoke, not search for the colonists in the Chesapeake Bay area, which had long been considered an alternative site—perhaps even better than the Outer Banks area? And, fully aware that a larger fleet with more men and supplies was following him, why did he decide not to wait for them but to return at once with all the provisions he had brought? Were the Indians hostile? Were the men impatient?

Grenville also seems to have been insensitive to Ralegh's plans. Undoubtedly, Sir Richard's interest in the colony was based more on its use in conjunction with privateering than with colonization. When Grenville sailed from Bideford about the first of May, 1586 (an earlier departure on April 16 was aborted when the vessels under his command ran aground on Bideford Bar), he was commanding a fleet of two large and five smaller vessels, with a complement of approximately 400 men. On his crossing to America, Grenville stopped a number of merchant vessels (even one English ship), confiscating their cargoes if he thought they were trading with the Spaniards. According to Spanish accounts, Grenville's party tried to capture and burn the town of Puerto Santo but were driven off by the infuriated inhabitants. On arriving at Port Ferdinando, according to the account of Grenville's pilot, he "found the said island deserted," with no trace of the 1585 colonists or of Ralegh's supply ship, but discovered only "the bodies of one Englishman and one Indian hanged"—evidence of some altercation between Ralegh's supply ship and hostile natives not mentioned by Hakluyt or any other account.

But Grenville's additional actions are puzzling and must have disappointed Ralegh. With the ships, men, and supplies in his custody, two logical options were open to Sir Richard. In the absence of the original colonists, he might have chosen a suitable site and once more left men and supplies to reestablish a colony for another year—either at Roanoke or at the site he favored on Chesapeake Bay. He was well able to leave a force as strong as the one he had landed the previous year. Or, with equal logic, he could have recognized the failure of the first venture and withdrawn completely, reserving men and supplies for a better-planned expedition for the following year. But the middle course he took was bound to fail. He left a corporal's guard of fifteen or eighteen men (according to different accounts), four cannons, small arms, and provisions for two years. Where a hundred men had failed, a score could not hope to succeed.

The only possible explanation is that Grenville wanted to save his forces to engage in raids upon Spanish shipping on the return voyage and also be able to report to Ralegh that English colonists maintained a presence on the mainland of America. But, once more, these were fruitless ambitions. On the return voyage, Grenville's party looked in vain for prizes to take but found none. By the time they reached the Azores, many of his crew were sick; the pilot Diaz wrote that thirty-four died. The fleet turned about to take on fresh water and fish from Newfoundland and then returned to the chase. This second time their luck was better, and they landed at Bideford in December with three Dutch and two Spanish prizes. Although their reinforcement of Ralegh's colony failed, they had again repaid the costs of the enterprise and left Ralegh and Grenville able to continue their efforts to colonize in the New World.

XIII. Preparation for the Second Colony

When the first colonists landed with Drake at Portsmouth in July, 1586, Ralegh was not there to greet them; he was in residence at his new estates in southern Ireland. During the long winter the colonists had spent in Virginia, Ralegh, ever the entrepreneur, was busy with other plans to augment his fortune. The idea of conquering the land by establishing colonies of Englishmen, which he had proposed for America, was equally plausible for the hostile land of Ireland. When he had been drafted to lead the Virginia colony, Ralph Lane was building an estate for himself in County Kerry. And, after transporting the colonists to Roanoke, Sir Richard Grenville had similar ideas. Grenville and Ralegh, therefore, joined forces to convince the queen to split up the greater portion of Munster, taken from the Irish insurgents, into estates for English colonists who could develop the country and maintain the peace. Once she had agreed to this idea, they became suitors for grants that they could develop. Grenville and his cousin, St. Leger, were given large tracts in Munster—lands that they had formerly held but from which they had been expelled during the James Fitzgerald (called Fitzmaurice) uprisings of 1569. Ralegh used his credit with the queen to acquire title to a tract of nearly 40,000 acres in eastern Cork and Waterford counties, centering on the old city of Youghal at the mouth of the Blackwater River and extending as far north as Lismore Castle.

By midsummer, 1586, when his special emissaries to Virginia, Thomas Harriot and John White, were ready to give him their personal reports, Ralegh was already listed as living in Youghal; and it was to this area that Harriot and White traveled to give him firsthand accounts of their winter in America. Tradition has it that Sir Walter had been made mayor of the town and was living in a house called Myrtle Grove (still called "Ralegh's house"). Irish development was so demanding that it is possible that it was the involvement of both Grenville and Ralegh in their new settlement activities that delayed the Roanoke relief vessels, to the distress of the colonists there. For most of the time of the first English settlements in Roanoke, Ralegh was shuttling back and forth among Ireland, the court, and the West

Country. In London he was soothing the queen, on whom his entire fortune rested; in Devon and Cornwall he was seeking ships, supplies, and settlers for his New World colony and recruiting men to settle his new Irish lands; and in Ireland he was, like all overseers, appeasing the Irish peasants, organizing his farms, and installing new herds, crops, and improved farming methods to fill his coffers and enrich his queen.

That Ralegh allied his Irish colonies with his Virginia colony is demonstrated by the way he interlocked their personnel. Lane, Grenville, and many of Sir Walter's own "cousins" were investors in both. Lane and Grenville had large holdings of their own, and recent research has demonstrated that both Thomas Harriot and John White were involved in Ireland after their return from America. Harriot was given a long lease on the confiscated Augustinian priory of Molanna on the island of Dair-Inis in the Blackwater River, two and one-half miles north of Youghal. That he actually lived there for a time is attested to by an official census of the residents of Ralegh's estates taken on May 12, 1589, and by the fact that he certified the survey of Ralegh's properties in the late autumn of 1586 and the spring of 1587.

John White also held lands in Ralegh's seignory, lands to which he retired following his activities in Virginia. Letters from White are addressed from "Newtown in Kilmore," which has escaped identification until Alec Wallace recently shed light on this address:

Many a Harriot scholar on pilgrimage to Molanna must have walked or driven through a village, without realizing that Ballynoe—Baile nua—is the Irish for Newtown! Ballynoe it was from the time of King John until 1450, and from the time of King James until the present day, and Newtown only when the English Church or the English undertakers were masters of Youghal. . . . In the annals of Youghal, the sale by Ralegh to Boyle of his Irish estates is recorded, and this particular section of it is described as "the decayed town of Tallaghe, together with the lands and villages of Kilmore." So here in the Ralegh heartland, only a few miles from Molanna Abbey, is a sixteenth century Newtown in Kilmore, and it is here that White must have lived.

The settler's life in Ireland was as harsh and demanding as life in savage America. It was during this same year, 1586, that John Hooker dedicated his "History of Ireland" for Holinshed's *Chronicles*, describing a barren, desolate, and miserable land:

[Following the Desmond wars] the common people, such as escaped the sword, all for the most part are perished with famine or fled the country. The land itself being very fertile, it waxed barren, yielding neither corn nor fruits; the pasture without cattle, and the air without fowl, and the whole province for the most part desolate and uninhabited, saving towns and cities, and finally nothing there to be seen but misery and desolation.

It was to this joyless land that Harriot and White came to give their reports on how Ralegh's plans for Virginia were faring after a year's direct experience. With Lane's report in hand and with the supplemental information brought by his own observers, Ralegh needed to take stock of his position. The reports of Lane, Harriot, and White raised questions concerning whether Roanoke was a safe harbor or supply depot for ships large enough to threaten the Spanish vessels they would face. The hostility of the coastal Indians and the failure of the land to furnish effortless living would make recruitment for the next colony even more difficult than for the first. But privately to Ralegh, White and Harriot must have been critical of Lane's management— both for his maintaining an organization primarily military rather than self-supporting and for his harsh treatment of, and even cruelty to, the natives. Again, they argued, it was necessary to counter the bad publicity Roanoke had been given with publications that would rekindle some of the glamour that had accompanied the first settlement. Harriot had prepared a detailed chronicle of the expedition and much information about the native culture; White, although he had lost many of his drawings, still had a large portfolio capable of presenting the red man in a sympathetic and friendly fashion. Ralegh, however, was reluctant to press these issues, preferring to let feeling subside before launching a new campaign. Thus, Harriot put aside his detailed account (which has disappeared, probably forever).

But Ralegh recognized that there were things to be done. To retain his Virginia rights he had to maintain a settlement of some sort there, as Grenville had attempted earlier. It was imperative that supplies and reinforcements be sent without delay. Lane still insisted that the "Cittie of Ralegh" should be located on the Chesapeake Bay, where the Indians were reported to be friendlier, the harbors were deeper and more protected, and pearls and precious metals were said to be commonplace. Harriot and White, one or both of whom had probably spent the winter in the Chesapeake area, concurred in the location of the city but felt that it should be a self-supporting, self-perpetuating community of English residents on American soil and not a military installation. Only those who were able to manage their lands and willing to work for their own maintenance should be selected as colonists. The colonists should be expected to live in harmony with their Indian neighbors, not to serve as their overloads. English culture (including Anglicanism) should gradually permeate the native culture and beliefs through education and example, not through force, as the Spanish had attempted to employ. Harriot and White contended that these views, although somewhat idyllic, would go further to ensure success than would a military presence and, with Ralegh as governor of Virginia and official representative of Elizabeth of England, could establish a solid foothold for a major English society in the New World.

As a result of these deliberations, a corporate body known as "The Governor and Assistants of the City of Ralegh in Virginia" was formed on January 7, 1587. Articles of incorporation do not exist, but coats of arms for the "City of Ralegh," for John White as "Governor" of the city, and for twelve "Assistants" were drawn up by the Garter King of Arms. That these plans were rather hastily drawn is shown by the fact that the names of the assistants were not all known to the herald. But from other documents, all may be identified. To assist White in the governance of the City of Ralegh were Roger Bailey, Ananias Dare, Christopher Cooper, Simon Fernandes, William Fullwood, Dionys Harvey, George Howe, John Nichols, James Platt, Roger Pratt, John Sampson, and Thomas Stevens. Of the twelve, nine accompanied White on the second colonial voyage; three—Fullwood, Nichols, and Platt—remained behind to act as factors of the company in London.

Little is known of how or from where the majority of recruits for the second colony were obtained. Since White was in charge and since his twelve assistants were all listed as being from London, it is likely that this is where he commenced his preparations. Free grants of land (Harriot says a minimum of 500 acres) were offered to each settler who promised to work it. That White was confident of the success of the colony is attested to by the fact that he enlisted as recruits members of his own family, Eleanor and Ananias Dare, with Eleanor already pregnant. Cuthbert White may also have been a relative. Another assistant, Dionys Harvey, brought with him to the colony his pregnant wife, Marjory, whose child was to be the second-born English citizen of the New World.

Unlike the earlier attempts, the effort to finance a colony in 1587 was not a major problem. Although the queen was still reluctant to assign royal money to any venture involving risk, several of her ministers were willing to contribute. Ralegh's "cousin," William Sanderson, solicited support from London merchants and risked much of his own capital; in addition, he underwrote Ralegh's obligations. Almost out of the blue, the queen, on March 17, 1587, granted to Ralegh all the forfeited lands of Anthony Babington, the executed traitor who had organized a conspiracy to murder Elizabeth and return Mary to the throne. Sir Walter, who previously had owned only a small patrimony in Devonshire, suddenly found himself one of England's richest landed gentry, holding estates in five English counties and leases of Durham House and estates in Ireland. He had achieved the position of wealth and power he had sought for the past half-dozen years, and this period marks what Edward Edwards, mid-nineteenth-century biographer of Ralegh and editor of his letters, says was "the highest point of mere favor to which Ralegh was able to climb." Ralegh's contribution at this juncture was limited only by his own caution, and he spared no effort to make his second colonial effort the best he could muster.

XIV. The Lost Colony of 1587

No episode in the history of America has captured the imagination of the American people more than the "Lost Colony" on Roanoke Island. Subject of vast historical research and multitudes of poems, novels, and plays, this romantic mystery is part of the nation's traditional heritage. For there was shattered Sir Walter Ralegh's dream—a permanent settlement of what was to become the British Empire and his thankful gift to the sovereign to whom he owed his entire fortune. The dream was a possible one, the plan was essentially sound, and hopes and ambitions ran high, both among the settlers themselves and those they left behind in their homeland. But a combination of events conspired to doom the enterprise: the Armada, the principal threat posed by the war with Spain; hazards of oceanic travel and sea piracy; fading determination and interest with the passing of time; and, it appears from the vantage point of the present time, lack of the essential qualities of leadership in those whom Ralegh had chosen to direct the activities and assume responsibility for their success.

It is almost paradoxical that Ralegh, whose powers of persuasion could always arouse the sympathy and enlist the support of those he could reach, was a poor judge of men when choosing for trust and responsibility. Those in whom he put the most trust (with the exception of Thomas Harriot) seemed most likely to let him down in moments of crisis. Lane (who may have been the choice of the queen instead of Sir Walter), John White, Lawrence Keymis, and even his beloved son and heir, Walter Ralegh the younger—none of these men demonstrated insight or good judgment under extreme difficulties and instead caused infinite pain and sorrow to the man they served and loved.

In many ways, the tragedy of the Lost Colony was more painful for John White than it was for Ralegh. In this failure, Sir Walter lost prestige, wealth, authority, and power. White's loss was greater: he lost friends whom he had persuaded to leave their homes and start a new life under his leadership; he lost all the personal possessions that he had selected to give him consolation in a foreign land; and he lost those most dear to him—his daughter Eleanor Dare, her husband Ananias, and his (so far as can be determined) only grandchild, Virginia Dare, the first English baby to be born in the wilderness for which she was named. But the bitterest aspect of all must have been White's recognition that these tragic losses were in part attributable to his own inadequacies as a leader, his inability to be firm when firmness was needed, and his lack of courage to follow plans in difficult times. Ralegh was but one man White disappointed; more important, he disappointed himself.

It was late April, 1587, when Governor White set sail on the fourth American voyage sponsored by Ralegh. The account of the crossing, told by White himself and published by Hakluyt two years later, reflects none of the drama and romance usually associated with the Lost Colony. White's account is disappointing—it leaves unanswered many questions of concern to its readers. Who were these colonists? What special skills did they have? What were their plans for life in the New World? What preparations had they made for a new life in a strange land? What special mementoes of home and family did they carry in the cramped space available on their three ships? What plans had they made for living with (and perhaps converting to Christianity) the Indians who would be their neighbors? The list goes on and on. But White, writing to Ralegh to justify his own return, gives none of the answers. His account is dry and factual, beginning:

Our fleet being in number three sails, viz the Admiral, a ship of one hundred and twenty tons, a Flyboat, and a Pinnace, departed the sixth and twentieth of April from Portsmouth, and the same day came to anchor at the Cowes in the Isle of Wight, where we stayed for eight days.

Why Portsmouth? Why the Isle of Wight? Why a delay of eight days there? No answer. The log continues:

The 5 of May, at nine of the clock at night, we came to Plymouth, where we remained for the space of two days.

The 8 we weighed anchor at Plymouth, and departed thence for Virginia.

The 16 Simon Fernandez, Master of our Admiral, lewdly forsook our Flyboat, leaving her distressed in the Bay of Portugal.

What might have been early disaster proved not to be: the admiral (the *Lion*) and the pinnace made a fast crossing, arriving at Dominica forty-two days after White departed Plymouth, and the abandoned flyboat followed only two days later.

Although White's narrative omits many items that would be of interest at the present time, it does reveal much about White himself.

He was named governor by Ralegh and given specific orders concerning how he was to proceed. Yet, it is obvious from White's account that he never really took command of the venture and was unable to persuade the assistants to follow the instructions he had been given. This initial brush with Fernandes, in which the pilot defied White's orders, was the first instance of the governor's lack of control of the expedition. It is obvious that the same animosity that had marked the feeling between Lane and Fernandes during the earlier expedition was present once more. Evidently, the two men were totally at cross purposes: White wanted to get to Virginia quickly in order to establish his colony during the summer months; Fernandes wanted to use the crossing to locate Spanish ships that might be seized for their cargoes. According to White, nothing could induce the pilot to accept orders, with results that were always detrimental. Fernandes sent men to look for water where there was none, to dig for salt where none existed, and to find sheep where they could not be found. Furthermore, he assured them that they were safe on islands later found to be overrun by cannibalistic Caribs. Even his navigation was faulty, as he mistook Cape Fear for Croatoan and almost wrecked the entire project. But the major insubordination occurred when the pilot refused to obey White's specific instructions to establish their colony at the new site on Chesapeake Bay. As they proceeded up the coast, White took the pinnace with forty of his best men to explore Roanoke, looking for the men left there by Grenville the previous year. This was to be, as White described it, a temporary excursion:

meaning after we had so done, to return again to the fleet and pass along the coast to the Bay of Chesapeake, where we intended to make our seat and fort, according to the charge given us among other directions in writing, under the hand of Sir Walter Ralegh: but as soon as we were put out with our pinnace from the ship, a Gentleman by the means of Fernandez, who was appointed to return to England, called to the sailors in the pinnace, charging them not to bring any of the planters back again, but leave them on the Island, except the Governor and two or three such as he approved, saying the Summer was far spent, wherefore he would land all the planters in no other place. . . .

Since this was on July 22, transoceanic shipping would not be hazardous for some time; obviously, Fernandes and his sailors knew that the Spanish fleet normally reached the Azores in late August or early September, and they were anxious to be there in wait for them. But the words of Fernandes spoke louder than the commands of Governor White: "Unto this were all the sailors, both in the Pinnace and ship, persuaded by the Master, wherefore it booted not the Governor to contend with them."

The visit to Roanoke Island was a great disappointment to White and his party:

When we came thither, we found the fort razed down, but all the houses standing unhurt, saving the nether rooms of them, and also of the fort, were overgrown with Melons of divers sorts, and Deer within them, feeding on those Melons: so we returned to our company, without hope of ever seeing any of the fifteen men living.

For some reason yet to be determined, White and his assistants quietly acceded to the decision made by Fernandes and settled down on Roanoke Island for a second attempt to found an English colony for Ralegh and the queen. The dangers of this location and the hostility already engendered in the neighboring Indians were quickly evident. Within the first week, one of the assistants, George Howe, ventured out alone to catch crabs. Mainland Indians, on Roanoke to hunt deer, sighted Howe and "shot at him in the water, where they gave him sixteen wounds with their arrows, and after they had slain him with their wooden swords, beat his head in pieces and fled over the water to the main." The Indians of nearby Croatoan Island were less belligerent: they told the settlers that the marauding savages were the remnants of the Wingina tribe, which had caused Lane's colonists such grief, and that they had likewise killed all the men left on the island by Grenville. From that time on, it was necessary to keep a sharp lookout day and night.

Two significant events occurred during these early days: on August 13 "our savage Manteo, by the commandment of Sir Walter Ralegh, was christened in Roanoke, called Lord thereof and of Dasemonkepeuc, in reward for his faithful service." This was the first recorded admission of a native American to the Church of England. Five days later, on Friday, August 18,

Eleanor, daughter to the Governor, and wife to Ananias Dare, one of the Assistants, was delivered of a daughter in Roanoke, and the same was christened there the Sunday following, and because the child was the first Christian born in Virginia, she was named Virginia. By this time our ships had unlanded the goods and victuals of the planters, and began to take in wood, and fresh water, and to new calk and trim them for England: the planters also prepared their letters, and tokens, to send back into England.

The season was growing late, and Fernandes was impatient to be on his way. On the day following the christening of Virginia Dare, a "northeaster" blew up and the ships were forced to cut their cables to stay in the open sea. Once again White's lack of leadership became evident. Although three of the assistants had remained in England to serve as factors for the colonists, there had been talk at the last minute in favor of sending two more assistants back to England with the ships to ensure continued availability of supplies. Obviously, there was disagreement between White and his council, and when he could not convince them, he acquiesced. But when he tried to name two to return, he ran into stiff opposition: no one wanted to leave his family, his newly acquired property, or his worldly possessions. The outcome was what might have been anticipated: the assistants unanimously agreed that White himself should go. White protested, but weakly and ineffectually, that his return would discredit him and the project. Furthermore,

he alleged, that seeing they intended to remove 50 miles further up into the main presently, he being then absent, his stuff and goods might be both spoiled, and most of it pilfered away in the carriage, so that at his return, he should be either forced to provide himself of all such things again, or else at his coming again to Virginia, find himself utterly unfurnished. . . . Wherefore he concluded, that he would not go himself.

Unfortunately, it seems characteristic of White that he was less concerned about his responsibilities as governor and his duty to oversee the development of Ralegh's colony than he was about his personal goods and his reputation. When the council insisted on his going, White demanded a formal contract to protect these interests, a document that David Quinn characterizes as "the first formal document to survive which originated in an English settlement on the mainland of North America." This document, dated August 25, 1587, and included as part of White's report to Ralegh on his return, required the assistants to guarantee restoration of his property if any of it was lost. Two days later, on August 27, one week after the christening of his granddaughter, White boarded the flyboat to return to England.

Ill fortune dogged White on his return. As the ship's crew raised the anchor to depart, one of the capstan crossbars broke; and before it could be stopped, it seriously injured twelve of the fifteen men aboard the flyboat. When the party arrived at the Azores it became apparent that Fernandes would not take the admiral back to England but would instead seek Spanish prizes. White and his disabled crew were on their own to sail for England. Then nature conspired against them when a storm blew for six days. With their fresh water depleted by a leak, the crew barely survived on beer and wine. With its crew lost and in devastated physical condition, the flyboat sailed on, until on October 16 land was sighted ("but we knew not what land it was") at Smerwick on the west coast of Ireland. White evidently was the healthiest man aboard; he arranged for delivery of fresh water, wine, and fruit, but for some it was too late. Within a week the steward, the boatswain, and the boatswain's mate died without leaving the vessel. White moved ashore the remainder of the crew, who were too sick to leave, and proceeded on to England, where he learned that Fernandes and the *Lion* had arrived three weeks earlier with no prizes but with crew so ill that they could not man their boats and had to be carried ashore.

White's report to Ralegh was a mixture of bad and good. The men left by Grenville in 1586 had all been driven off by hostile natives. The ocean lanes had proved more hazardous than had earlier been believed, and the possibility of tragedy from frequent northeasters was evident. But on the positive side, a new kind of colony, dedicated to self-sufficiency and prepared for the hard work necessary for survival, had been established for the first time, and life had begun to assume a normal routine. None of the settlers was willing to return to England, so morale obviously was high; and the Virginian English, once supplies were assured, would have a firm colonial foothold in the New World. In that, Sir Walter Ralegh could take comfort.

XV. Plans to Resupply the White Colony

John White took seriously his charge to obtain fresh supplies for his colonists, but the same ill fortune that had plagued his return voyage continued to frustrate him. By the time he met with Ralegh on November 20, 1587, England was already engaged in preparations for a Spanish invasion of its mainland. War was fully expected; indeed, it was the English who had forced the issue and made the first overt acts of aggression, far beyond occasional piratical raids on the Spanish Atlantic fleet. Most of the knowledgeable members of Elizabeth's inner circle believed that an all-out war with Spain was inevitable even before White sailed in the spring of 1587. By the time he returned, they were certain.

It was the hot-headed English naval commander Sir Francis Drake who opened the conflict. Incited by the Babington plot to murder Elizabeth, her excommunication by Rome, and the critical stage of the Protestant-Catholic warfare in the Netherlands, and bolstered by the success of his raids against Spanish cities in middle and southern America, Drake prepared for a direct assault on Cadiz. The queen contributed four huge new warships built by John Hawkins, another English naval commander—the *Elizabeth Bonaventure,* the *Golden Lion,* the *Dreadnought,* and the *Rainbow.* English merchants contributed eight more. On April 2 Drake, in the flagship *Elizabeth Bonaventure,* sailed from Plymouth to Cadiz, where it was known that a huge aggregation of Spanish ships was being outfitted, ostensibly for the invasion of England. On April 3 he sailed his fleet into the outer harbor, where the shipping and supply boats lay anchored, shooting, burning, and looting almost at will. The following day he entered the inner harbor, where the commander-designate of the Armada, the Marquis of Santa Cruz, was refitting his huge war galleons. By the time that day was done, the English had wrought terrific destruction on a major arm of the Spanish fleet. According to Drake's own count, thirty-seven ships had been sunk, burned, or captured.

Nevertheless, this did not assuage Drake's anger. For several weeks he sailed up and down the Spanish coast, destroying vessels laden with supplies for Spain and capturing shore bases for his own supply. He then learned that a great carrack from the East Indies was approaching the Azores. Never one to resist such temptations, Drake immediately sailed out to capture that great vessel and its cargo. The ship, the *San Felipe,* proved to be the property of the king of Spain, and it carried a cargo valued at more than £114,000. Drake's seizure of this prize more than covered the total cost of the Cadiz venture, with a profit left over for the queen and all the investors. Drake returned to England once more a hero: the Spaniards' plan for invasion was deferred for at least a year, and the English could take great pride that Drake had succeeded beyond their fond hopes. He had "singed the King of Spain's beard!"

This action, however, left no doubt that King Philip would invade England as quickly as his forces could be put in order. On October 9, 1587, therefore, even before White had landed in Ireland, England's Privy Council issued an order staying all shipping out of British ports in order that all naval support could be mustered immediately in the event of the expected attack. Nevertheless, White and Ralegh continued to plan for the relief of the Roanoke settlers. White was to outfit a pinnace with supplies and be prepared to leave as soon as weather and winds would permit. Grenville was again to furnish a large support force of seven or eight vessels that would carry enough arms to defend the colonists from any Spanish attack in that area and undoubtedly would seek prizes as they did so.

By February, 1588, White had outfitted and supplied two small vessels. One of these ships was the *Brave,* a 30-ton bark that carried seven men and two women as additions to the permanent colony, as well as meal, vegetables, and biscuits for the settlers; the *Brave* carried Pedro Diaz as pilot, Arthur Facy as captain, and Governor White himself. Also ready to depart was another vessel, the 25-ton *Roe,* about which little is known except that it carried four or five additional colonists. Grenville had secured access to the 250-ton galleon *Dudley,* the 200-ton *Virgin, God Save Her,* the *Tiger,* the *Golden Hind,* the *St. Leger,* and some small-draft ships. Early in 1588 these vessels were in port awaiting favorable winds when news of their imminent departure reached London. On March 31 the Privy Council took action, commanding Grenville "in Her Majesty's name and upon his allegiance to forbear to go on his intended voyage, and to have the ships so by him prepared to be in readiness to join with Her Majesty's navy as he shall be directed hereafter." Specific orders followed nine days later: Grenville was to turn over all his major vessels to Sir Francis Drake at Plymouth; the ships were to be used for the defense of England against the forthcoming Armada from Spain. The smaller and poorly armed vessels, however, "he might dispose of and employ in his intended voyage."

It was as a result of these orders, then, that on April 22, 1588, Governor White, in "two small pinnaces, the one of them being of 30 tons" [the *Brave*], the other the *Roe*, "wherein 15 planters and all their provision, with certain relief for those that wintered in the Country," sailed from Bideford, Cornwall; the two vessels were all that could be salvaged from the efforts of White, Grenville, and Ralegh.

For Ralegh, White, the new settlers, and the Virginia colonists, White's 1588 relief voyage was an unmitigated disaster. Although White's counsel had been heeded and Simon Fernandes was not to pilot this voyage, the naming of Arthur Facy as captain of the flagship *Brave* was an equally costly blunder. Facy had been one of Grenville's masters in the 1585 voyage, during which he had shown himself to be an uncontrollable privateer. According to White's later account of this voyage (printed by Hakluyt the following year), Facy commenced his raiding action even before the *Brave* departed the coast of England. One day after weighing anchor, White wrote, while still in sight of land, the *Brave* chased four ships and searched them for loot. The following day they boarded two more ships—one a Scot and the other a Breton—and Facy "took from them whatsoever he could find worth the taking, and so let them go." On April 29 the tiny *Roe* attacked a "hulk of 200 tons and more," borrowing men and ammunition from the *Brave* to maintain the attack until the vessel got too close to the Spanish coast and thus escaped.

On May 5, near the island of Madeira, the two small pinnaces encountered a pair of French men-of-war, "well manned and bravely," and bound for Peru. Although the English resorted to both friendly manners and flight, they were attacked by the overpowering French. The resulting battle, a death knell to White's hopes for the voyage and of dire significance to the Roanoke colonists, is best told in the unemotional but graphic words of John White himself.

The next morning being Monday and the 6. of May, we escried them in the weather of us, so that it was in vaine to seeke by flight, but rather by fight to helpe our selves. The same day about 2. of the clocke in the afternoone they were come with us. We hayled them, but they would not answere. Then we waved them to leewardes of us, and they waved us with a sword amayne, fitting their sailes to clappe us aboord, which we perceiving gave them one whole side: with one of our great shot their Master gonners shoolder was stroken away, and our Master gonner with a small bullet was shot into the head. Being by this time grappled and aboord each of other the fight continued without ceasing one houre and a halfe. In which fight were hurt & slaine on both sides 23. of the chiefest men, having most of them some 6. or 8. woundes, and some 10. or 12. woundes. Being thus hurt and spoiled they robbed us of all our victuals, powder, weapons and provision, saving a smal quantity of biskuit to serve us scarce for England. Our Master and his Mate were deadly wounded, so that they were not able to come forth of their beds. I my selfe was wounded twise in the head, once with a sword, and another time with a pike, and hurt also in the side of the buttoke with a shot. Three of our passagers were hurt also, whereof one had 10. or 12. woundes our Master hurt in the face with a pike and thrust quite through the head. Being thus put to our close fights, and also much pestred with cabbens and unserviceable folkes we could not stirre to handle our weapons nor charge a piece: againe having spent all the powder in our flaskes and charges which we had present for our defence, they cut downe our netting and entred so many of their men as could stand upon our poope and forecastle, from whence they played extreemely upon us with their shot. As thus we stood resolved to die in fight, the Captaine of the Frenchmen cried to us to yeld and no force should be offred. But after we had yelded, they knowing so many of their best men to be hurt and in danger of present death, began to grow into a new furie, in which they would have put us to the sword had not their Captaine charged them, and persuaded them to the contrary. Being at length pacified they fell on all handes to rifling and carying aboord all the next day until 4. of the clock: at which time by over greedy lading both their owne boate and ours, they sunke the one and split the other by the ships side: by meanes whereof they left us two cables and ankers, all our ordinance and most part of our sailes, which otherwise had ben taken away also. Furthermore they doubting the wind would arise, and night at hand, & a tal ship al that day by meanes of the calme in sight, they came aboord us with their ship, and tooke in their men that were in us, who left us not at their departing any thing worth the carying away. Being thus ransacked and used as is aforesaid in all sorts, we determined (as our best shift in so hard a case) to returne for England, and caused all our able and unhurt men, to fal to newe rigging & mending our sailes, tacklings, and such things as were spilled in our fight. By this occasion, God justly punishing our former theeverie of our evil desposed mariners, we were of force constrained to break of our voyage intended for the reliefe of our Colony left the yere before in Virginia, and the same night to set our course for England, being then about 50. leagues to the Northeast of Madera.

On May 22 the shattered party of the *Brave* returned to Cornwall. There, awaiting high tide, they crossed over the bar and landed at Bideford, where, White reported, the *Roe* joined them a few weeks later "without performing our intended voyage for the relief of the planters in Virginia, which therby were not a little distressed." Relief efforts in 1588 had produced no good results; financially they were a total loss for both White and Ralegh. It is likely that the fiasco sealed the fate of the 1587 White colony.

XVI. The Armada, 1588

Records are inadequate to allow Sir Walter Ralegh's activities during the frenzied preparations for the Spanish invasion of England to be examined. His was certainly not a principal role, as were those of Howard, Drake, or Hawkins, but as a member of the council of war, named by the queen, he had a voice in the general planning for the national defense. Years later, in his *Historie of the World,* he took credit for the hit-and-run strategy that gave the English their monumental victory, but his role is not mentioned in other sources. He also made an important contribution in ships: the *Ark Royal,* the tremendous warship chosen by Howard as the flagship of the defenses and which led the action during the fray, was the renamed *Ark Ralegh,* built by Sir Walter in 1586 for privateering and given to the queen for her Royal Navy out of gratitude for her grant of the Babington estates. Ralegh's *Roebuck,* too, was an especially effective warship and won recognition for its activities in fighting the huge carracks of the Armada.

During the spring of 1588, while White was preparing for his departure, all Englishmen were mobilized for the attack they knew was coming. Ralegh, sensitive to the vulnerability of the long coastline and good harborages of the West Country, was busy improving the defenses of Cornwall and Devon. The Privy Council had recommended that Sir Walter raise 2,000 soldiers and 20 cavalry to repel any attack, but he felt more men were needed. As lord warden of the Stannaries and lord lieutenant of Cornwall, Ralegh had access to the local parliaments and often met with them to elicit their support. He raised much larger forces than requested, armed them handsomely, implemented training programs, and established a rendezvous headquarters at Plymouth, which was recognized as a particularly vulnerable port for debarkation of the Spanish armies. Having thus prepared, Ralegh returned to Ireland, where his new estates were demanding his attention.

Ralegh was in Youghal on July 19 when the Armada was sighted in the English Channel advancing on Plymouth. Bonfires and church bells carried the warning, and all England was mobilized for action

At Ralegh's suggestion, Lord High Admiral Charles Howard of Effingham concentrated England's naval forces at Plymouth and led a heroic effort that resulted in the repulsion of the Spanish Armada from the English Channel. Engraving from Edmund Lodge, *Portraits of Illustrious Personages of Great Britain* (London: William Smith, 12 volumes in 8, 1835), IV.

overnight. Lord High Admiral Charles Howard of Effingham, who had concentrated his naval forces at Plymouth as Ralegh had suggested, immediately led his ships out of the harbor, determined to prevent the Spanish from landing troops in the south of England. Although outnumbered in ships and outmanned in fighting personnel, Howard and his major admirals—Sir John Hawkins, Sir Martin Frobisher, and Sir Francis Drake—utilized fully the one major advantage they had over the invading navy. The English warships, especially those designed by Hawkins, were longer and lower than the high-decked enemy vessels. Lying low in the water, they presented less of a target to enemy guns; they were also quicker to respond and could sail closer to the wind than the unwieldy Spanish galleons. Howard and his forces quickly got on the windward side of the Armada fleet, ranged in an advancing crescent, and, avoiding the trap of attacking the middle, concentrated on hit-and-run attacks on the extremities. For nearly a week they alternately attacked and withdrew, while the west-southwest wind gradually moved the entire battle fleet along the south coast of England.

News of the invasion spread to Ireland, and Ralegh left at once for England. His role in the actual naval battle remains uncertain: many of his biographers confidently assert that he commanded one of the ships engaged in active fighting throughout the decisive periods of battle; others are less sure. In all his writings, Ralegh nowhere indicates that he was directly involved. And although the official rosters

63

are filled with the names of his friends and associates, nowhere in the records is Sir Walter mentioned. According to Spanish accounts, it was Ralegh who on July 25 carried from Queen Elizabeth to Admiral Howard the message ordering Howard "to attack the Armada in some way, or to engage it if he could not burn it." Although it would be pleasant to picture Sir Walter as active in the defense of his country, it is most likely that he was either in attendance at court or continuing his mobilization of the West Country during the critical weeks of the conflict—the week of battle across the south of England, the final foray of fire ships, and the frenzied attack of July 28-29 that forced the disrupted Spanish forces through the Channel and northward up the coast, where the tempestuous storms could bring their final havoc to the bewildered invaders.

With the northward flight of the Armada, Ralegh returned to Ireland to assist Grenville in preparing to intercept any forces that might try to land in that Catholic country. But this was not to be: the Spanish who survived the terrific storms of the northern seas were sick of war and anxious to return home. Unexpectedly, the Irish proved hostile to any who were wrecked on their shores. By Christmas, Ralegh was back in London, again in attendance at court.

The actions of the returned John White during this time cannot be documented. Ralegh was too involved in other affairs to think much of his Virginia colonists, and White had no resources of his own to support relief of his family or friends. It is probable that it was at this time that White accepted a grant of land in Ralegh's Irish estates and began the hard life of an English planter in that desolate and war-torn wilderness. But early in 1589 White and Ralegh began again to seek broader support for the Virginia settlers. They proposed to open up the commercial possibilities of the new American lands in exchange for financial backing of the colony there. On May 7, 1589, a tripartite agreement was drawn among Ralegh, the assistants of the City of Ralegh, and a consortium of nineteen London merchants as associates in the enterprise. As reward for their support of the Virginia colony, the new associates were to be granted free trade between Virginia and England for seven years without payment of any dues or taxes; the assistants and the colonists they represented were to receive food and supplies and free shipping for their goods; and Ralegh, still retaining all his rights to establish other colonies, was to receive one fifth of all gold and silver, or ore, shipped from America. The names of the London merchants as given by Hakluyt constituted an impressive listing, including such wealthy and respected traders as Thomas Smith and William Sanderson, the herbalist John Gerrard, the mathematical lecturer Thomas Hood, Richard Hakluyt, and Richard Wright (who was later to be influential in the East India Company). It is exceedingly difficult to understand why, with the support of this group, ships, men, and supplies were not forthcoming and why no concrete action to implement the agreement was taken during the whole of 1589.

It is possible that Ralegh himself was not inclined to push the matter as he might have been expected to do. He may have been engaged in the critically dangerous (for one of the queen's favorites) business of wooing one of the ladies of the court. Pierre Lefranc, the modern French biographer of Ralegh, has uncovered lawsuits suggesting that Ralegh's marriage to Elizabeth Throckmorton (Lady Bess) actually took place in secret on February 20, 1588—although it was apparently a secret until 1592. Nothing in the record rules out this possibility, and if true it explains some of the enigmatic passages in the later letters of both Sir Walter and Lady Bess. Such a romance would have complicated the life of an already aging suitor who was being superseded in the queen's affection by the dashing young earl of Essex. It was during August, 1589, that Sir Francis Allen wrote to Anthony Bacon, an English diplomat then in Europe, that "My Lord of Essex has chased Mr. Ralegh from the Court, and hath confined him into Ireland." And this was the autumn that Ralegh visited the poet Edmund Spenser at Spenser's Irish estate at Kilkolman, traded verses with him, and first read the early cantos of *The Faerie Queene*. Whatever the cause, Ralegh and White passed this entire year without further involvement in the New World.

XVII. White's Last Voyage, 1590

More than a decade had passed since Sir Walter Ralegh had first sailed on the abortive expedition of the winter of 1578-1579 and experienced for the first time the tribulations of sea warfare and stormy weather. During these ten years, more than a quarter of his life, Virginia and the development of a colonial empire in Virginia had dominated his interests and exerted first claim on his recently acquired wealth. Although the fondness of the queen had denied him his ambition to participate directly in the founding of a new England, he had unstintingly furnished ships, recruited sailors and settlers, and stocked food and supplies for the lengthy ocean voyages and the long, unproductive winters faced by the settlers. Nevertheless, returns from these enterprises had been minimal. Ralegh had obtained from the Indians tobacco and pipes in which to smoke it, and he had converted many of the court to the new habit of smoking, which he proclaimed conducive to health and longevity. Sweet-smelling cedar wood had become popular in London (Sir Walter gave a bed of it to his friend Henry Percy, ninth earl of Northumberland, in February, 1587), and the bark of the sassafras was being imported to cure syphilis brought back to Europe by the Spanish. But these were trivial returns for tremendous investment. In fact, the only American activity that had paid Ralegh handsome dividends was the privateering, which had interfered so greatly with the colonizing efforts of both Lane and White. Although it is difficult if not impossible to estimate the returns from this activity, it is more than likely that these spoils repaid Ralegh and the other investors in full—perhaps with a handsome profit added. It must be reckoned only natural, therefore, that priority was frequently given to the support of privateering rather than colonization.

John White thought differently. Although his resources had been strained by his previous voyages, he felt strongly his responsibilities as governor both to the settlers and to the personal family he had left in the New World. Although he was unable to finance another relief expedition, he nevertheless sought other opportunities to get supplies to the Roanoke colonists. In January, 1590, he thought he saw just such a chance. Master John Watts, a London merchant who was a most avid privateer, was gathering a fleet in the Thames and was, as White wrote to Hakluyt, "absolutely determined to go for the West Indies." Watts had three heavily armed warships ready to sail when the Privy Council, fearing another Spanish invasion, once more ordered all merchant shipping to remain in port. In these circumstances, White saw an opportunity: he immediately got in touch with Sir Walter to seek his help in getting the queen to intervene and to permit the vessels to depart if they would land White, his supplies, and new colonists at Roanoke on the way to the West Indies. In this endeavor Ralegh was successful, and Watts posted bond to deliver White and his relief expedition in Virginia.

Again, these were false promises. Even before their departure, Watts showed himself to be a villain. As White complained to Hakluyt, "in contempt of the aforesaid order, I was by the owner and commanders of the ships denied to have any passengers, or anything else, transported in any of the said ships, saving only myself and my chest." When White wanted to inform Ralegh of this, the captains protested that they were ready to sail and would go without him. It was the same old story: White wanted to go to Roanoke; the seamen wanted to take prizes, being, in White's words, "wholly disposed themselves to seek after purchase and spoils, spending so much time therein that summer was spent before we arrived at Virginia."

It was on March 20, 1590, that White, alone in his concern for the colonists and without supplies, sailed from Plymouth harbor on the Watts flagship *Hopewell*. And it was not until August 15 that the coast of Virginia was sighted: "towards evening we came to an anchor at Hatarask [Port Ferdinando] . . . three leagues from shore." The crew's first view was encouraging—they sighted smoke near the site of the colony. The night of August 15 was filled with anticipation for White, who was anxious to meet again with his friends.

The 16 [August] and next morning, our two boats went ashore, and Captain Cocke[3] and Captain Spicer[4] and their company with me, with intent to pass to the place at Roanoke where our countrymen were left. At our putting from the ship we commanded our master gunner to make ready two minions and a falcon well loaded, and to shoot them off with reasonable space between every shot, to the end that their reports might be heard to the place where we hoped to find some of our people.

But the anticipated meeting was again delayed. Their two small boats came closer to shore, taking soundings as they came, when

67

before we were half way between our ships and the shore, we saw another great smoke to the southwest of Kenricks Mounts:[5] we therefore thought good to go to that second smoke first, but it was much further from the harbor where we landed than we supposed it to be, so that we were very sore tired before we came to the smoke. But that which grieved us more was that when we came to the smoke we found no man nor sign that any had been there lately, nor yet any fresh water in all this way to drink. Being thus wearied with this journey, we returned to the harbor where we left our boats. . . . That night we returned aboard with our boats and our whole company in safety.

White remained buoyed by the thought that the following day would bring a reunion at Roanoke, still twenty miles to the north. But the weather, which had been foul since the first of August, suddenly turned worse, and a northeaster started to raise high waves in the shallow waters of Port Ferdinando. Before starting for Roanoke, Captain Spicer insisted that the ship's potable water be replenished, so it was after ten o'clock in the morning before they were ready to depart. Although the seas were high, Captain Cocke's boat, carrying White, landed safely; nevertheless, supplies, food, matches, and powder were soaked. The second boat, with Captain Spicer and his men, was less fortunate. White's account is, as usual, simple and unemotional:

Captain Spicer came to the entrance of the breach with his mast standing up, and was half passed over, but by the rash and indiscreet steerage of Ralph Skinner, his master's mate, a very dangerous sea broke into their boat and overset them quite. The men kept [to] the boat, some in it and some hanging on it, but the next sea set the boat aground, where it beat so that some of them were forced to let go their hold, hoping to wade ashore, but the sea still beat them down so that they could neither stand nor swim, and the boat twice or thrice was turned the keel upward. Whereupon Captain Spicer and Skinner hung until they sunk and [were] seen no more. But four more that could swim a little kept themselves in deeper water and were saved by Captain Cocke's means, who so soon as he saw their oversetting, stripped himself and four others that could swim very well, and with all haste possible rowed unto them and saved four. They were eleven in all, and seven of the chiefest were drowned, whose names were Edward Spicer, Ralph Skinner, Edward Kelley, Thomas Bevis, Hance the Surgeon, Edward Kelborne, [and] Robert Coleman.

Consternation over this loss was great, and the men were most reluctant to proceed to Roanoke but finally agreed. The two boats were refitted, and the nineteen remaining men proceeded up the sound toward Roanoke, which White had left just ten days less than three years previously.

Most of the day had passed, and it was so dark when they reached the island that the men of the expedition almost overshot it. But, passing the north end in the dark, they once more spied a great fire, which they felt certain was a signal set by the colonists. Although it was too dark to attempt a landing, the two boats drew near the light, anchored, and in high spirits "sounded with a trumpet a call, and afterwards many familiar English tunes of songs, and called to them friendly; but we had no answer."

The night was long for the impatient White, but as soon as it was dawn the boats landed on the nearest shore and the men moved quickly to the fire. Once more they were disappointed, for "coming to the fire, we found the grass and sundry rotten trees burning about the place"—evidence of the effects of the lightning that accompanied the recent storms (just as the fire at Kenricks Mounts had been). Although the men were anxious to leave, White for once was insistent that the search be thorough. They left the boats on the northeast coast and walked in a southwesterly direction across the island, arriving on the west side across from the Indian village of Dasemunkepeuc. Finding no evidence of occupation, they retraced their steps along the northern coastline "until we came to the place where I left our Colony in the year 1587," possibly near the site of the present Fort Raleigh. There White expected to find his friends (if they had remained at Roanoke)—or at least information as to where they had gone. White's description of his findings is succinct but sad:

In all this way we saw in the sand [only] the print of the Savage's feet of two or three sorts, trodden that night, and as we entered up the sandy bank, upon a tree in the very brow thereof, were curious carved these fair Roman letters C R O: which letters presently we knew to signify the place where I should find the planters seated, according to a secret token agreed between them and me at my last departure from them, which was that in any ways they should not fail to write or carve on the trees or posts of the doors the name of the place where they should be seated, for at my coming away they were prepared to remove from Roanoke fifty miles into the main. . . .

It is not clear from his account or any account just what plans the 1587 colonists had for a permanent settlement. They may have attempted to follow Ralegh's plan for a site on the Chesapeake, where better harborage and more protection from possible Spanish raids was available. Or they may have felt it better to settle on the banks of the Albemarle Sound or the Chowan River, as Lane had urged.

But in any case, Roanoke was to be their rendezvous site, and White fully expected a message informing him where the colonists had gone or warning him if they were in trouble:

at my departure from them in Anno 1587 I willed them that if they should happen to be distressed in any of those places, that then they should carve over the letters or name, a Cross . . . , but we found no such sign of distress.

Some concern must have been felt, however, at the fact that there was only partial carving of a place name, indicating haste. White and his men hurried on to the site of the village.

having well considered of this, we passed toward the place where they were left in sundry houses, but we found the houses taken down, and the place very strongly enclosed with a high palisade of great trees, with curtains and flankers very fortlike. And one of the chief trees of posts at the right side of the entrance had the bark taken off, and five feet from the ground in fair capital letters was graven CROATOAN without any cross or sign of distress.

This gave some relief as White proceeded into the fort to see what evidence, if any, had been left for him there.

We entered into the palisade where we found many bars of iron, two pigs of lead, four iron fowlers [light ship cannons], iron saker-shot [small cannon shot], and such like heavy things, thrown here and there, almost overgrown with grass and weeds. From thence we went along by the water-side, toward the point of the creek, to see if we could find any of their boats or pinnaces, but we could perceive no sign of them, nor any of the last falcons and small ordnance which were left with them. . . .

From the evidence available, it appeared that the planters had left Roanoke in good order, taking with them things easily transportable in small boats and leaving heavy objects of doubtful value. The next discovery seemed also to bear this out:

At our return from the creek, some of our sailors, meeting us, told us that they had found where divers chests had been hidden, and long since dug up again and broken up, and much of the goods in them spoiled and scattered about, but nothing left of such things as the Savages knew any use of undefaced. Presently, Captain Cocke and I went to the place, which was in the end of an old trench, made two years past [that is before his last visit, or 1585] by Captain Amadas, where we found five chests that had been carefully hidden by the planters. And of the same chests three were my own [left under warranty in 1587], and about the place many of my things spoiled and broken, and my books torn from their covers, the frames of some of my pictures and maps rotten and spoiled with rain, and my armor almost eaten through with rust. This could be no other but the deed of the Savages, our enemies at Dasemunkepeuc, who had watched the departure of our men to Croatoan, and as soon as they had departed, [had] dug up every place where they suspected anything to be buried.

From the anguish White had exhibited on leaving these possessions in 1587, it might be assumed that he would be despondent over their recovery in such state. But surprisingly, he saw this as a positive indication that all was well with his colony:

although it grieved me to see such spoil of my goods, yet on the other side, I greatly joyed that I had safely found a certain token of their safe being at Croatoan, which is the place where Manteo was born, and the savages of the island our friends. . . . When we had seen in this place so much as we could, we returned to our boats and departed from the shore toward our ships with as much speed as we could, for the weather began to overcast, and very likely that a foul and stormy night would ensue.

It was a foul and stormy night, and the vile weather continued on the following day. Captain Cocke agreed to take White on to Croatoan to continue his search, but the heavy seas made maneuvering difficult if not impossible. Two anchors and cables were lost before the vessels got under way, "and the weather grew to be fouler and fouler, our victuals scarce, and our cask and fresh water lost." The attempt was finally abandoned, and White and Cocke decided to winter in the West Indies and to make another attempt to reach Croatoan the following spring. Captain John Bedford, who took command of the *Moonlight* when Spicer was drowned, rejected this idea and set sail for England without them.

But Cocke's crew was still interested in privateering. On the way to Trinidad, they changed course for the Azores, chasing Spanish vessels but capturing none. Finally, disheartened, they changed course for home. It was on October 24 that the *Hopewell* entered Plymouth Harbor and White prepared to make his last report to Sir Walter and to retire from public life to his estate in Ireland.

That White was despondent over his failure to aid the colony he governed goes without saying. In response to Hakluyt's request for a report on his fifth voyage (for Hakluyt's *Voyages*), White complied with the detailed narrative quoted so extensively in this chapter. But he also enclosed a final letter to Hakluyt—the last record of Governor White that exists—which ends with a poignant prayer:

Thus may you plainly perceive the success of my fifth and last voyage to Virginia, which was no less unfortunately ended than frowardly begun, and as luckless to many, as sinister to myself. But I would to God it had been as prosperous to all as noisome to the planters, and as joyful to me as discomfortable to them. Yet seeing it is not my first crossed voyage, I remain contented. And wanting [lacking] my wishes, I leave off from prosecuting that whereunto I would to God my wealth were answerable to my will. Thus committing the relief of my discomfortable company, the planters in Virginia, to the merciful help of the Almighty, whom I most humbly beseech to help and comfort them according to His most holy will and their good desire, I take my leave from my house at Newtown in Kilmore, the 4 of February, 1593.

XVIII. Ralegh Looks Southward

It was during the 1590s that Ralegh found himself tossed like fortune's tennis ball from high to low in both personal respect and fortune. John White's failure to find and strengthen his colonial settlement was but one of the many disappointments he was to face. The rise of his young rival Essex in the favor of the queen was undermining his influence at court and pinching off the flow of perquisites on which he had come to depend. But just as things were looking blackest for Ralegh, Essex married Frances, the widow of Sir Philip Sidney and daughter of Walsingham. Elizabeth, almost pathological about the marriage of one of her favorites, refused to accept this marriage. Essex had disgraced them all, she declared, by wedding beneath his station, and she shipped him off to the Continent as lord general in the wars between Henry of Navarre and the Catholics under Philip II of Spain. Ralegh once more found himself in favor and in wealth.

To cause discomfort to Philip, the Privy Council took official action to send English warships to the Azores to intercept the Spanish Plate Fleet, which was furnishing the wealth to conduct the king's religious wars. Lord High Admiral Charles Howard, who had led the English forces in the defeat of the Armada, was to lead this expedition. For this enterprise, Ralegh gladly furnished his *Bark Ralegh* to serve as Howard's flagship and provisioned two other vessels, including the *Revenge,* which he hoped to command himself. But as before, Elizabeth refused at the last minute to let him leave the court, and his place was taken by his cousin, Sir Richard Grenville, who had played such a large role in Ralegh's sea campaigns.

Like many others, this expedition seemed ill fated. Foul weather so delayed the English in departing that the Spanish learned of their plans and sent more than fifty of their newest and fastest warships to defend their royal gold and silver. Once again illness plagued the English crews, and by the time they reached the Azores only about half the seamen and soldiers were above decks. The resulting battle could have had only one outcome. Outnumbered in ships by more than three to one and outmanned even more, the English were soundly beaten, but only after one of the most famous sea battles in history.

Sir Richard Grenville, one of Sir Walter Ralegh's cousins, acted as "generall" during the colonizing voyage to Roanoke in 1585. His lengthy military career, and his life, ended in the Azores in 1591 during a heroic naval engagement with the Spanish. Engraving from copy in North Carolina Collection.

Especially heroic was the fight of Grenville in the *Revenge* against overwhelming odds.

Cut off from the rest of the fleet while acting as rear admiral, Grenville found his lone vessel facing five massive Spanish galleons. Refusing to turn, he sailed directly at them, firing at point-blank range while receiving both cannon and musket shot in return. Amid almost unbelievable carnage, the English, cheered on by Grenville, continued fighting for almost fifteen hours. Little remained of their ship: it had received more than 800 direct hits, many below the waterline; it had lost all its masts and the main deck was covered with its rigging and broken spars; more than half its men, hale and ill, had been killed. Still Grenville, sorely wounded himself, fought on. Two of the huge galleons were sunk and more than a thousand Spaniards slain by his handful of men. When it was possible to fight no longer and Grenville was planning to blow up his ship, the Spanish admiral, moved to admiration for the bravery of the English, sent lenient terms for surrender: no one would be killed—common soldiers and seamen would be returned to England, and gentlemen would be held in honor until ransomed. Against Grenville's pleas, his men accepted these terms, and the Spanish took what was left of the *Revenge*—the first English ship to be captured by Spain during the war. Taken aboard the enemy flagship, Grenville died three days later. According to the legend of the time, his last words were: "Here die I, Richard Grenville, with a joyful and quiet mind, having ended my life like a true soldier that has fought for his country, Queen, religion, and honor."

English loss from this expedition was great, both in money and in pride, and there was much grumbling about an unaccustomed defeat by King Philip's men. But very shortly appeared a resounding account of the battle that portrayed the heroic efforts of a few sturdy men as a victory in defeat. This was *A Report of the Truth of the Fight about the Isles of Azores,* published anonymously but widely recognized as having been written by Sir Walter as a means of paying his debt to a close friend who had lost his life as his stand-in as rear admiral to the English fleet. This fiery pamphlet roused England once again against the Spanish by portraying an epic spirit that inspired pride and patriotism—and has continued to do so to this day. It shows Ralegh at his most magnificent persuasiveness and makes clear how the man could so strongly influence those in his presence. And it again increased Ralegh's favor with the queen. In January, 1592, Elizabeth at long last acceded to Sir Walter's request: she leased him the manor of Sherborne in Dorset—the estate he called his "Castle" and on which he could lavish his architectural and landed ambitions to make the manor his patrimony for his family for generations to come.

In the spring of 1592 Ralegh continued to press for further onslaughts against the Spanish treasure ships. He convinced the queen that she should place him in command of another raiding fleet, this time to emulate Drake in attacking Spanish settlements in the Isthmus of Panama. With her agreement he named Sir John Burrough as his second-in-command, recruited a dozen ships, and, borrowing heavily, manned and outfitted them for a long voyage. But as usual, at the very last minute, Elizabeth refused Ralegh the personal command he sought. He could accompany the fleet for its first fifty or sixty leagues, she agreed, but then he must turn over command to Sir Martin Frobisher and return to her side. On the day after the raiding fleet left port, Frobisher arrived and ordered Ralegh to return. Ralegh refused, saying he had permission to go further. As they argued, they halted a Spanish ship and released an English captive, who gave them the bad news that the Plate Fleet was not to sail that year. Ralegh hastily revised his plans and decided to split the fleet. Half the vessels, under Frobisher, would proceed to the Azores to intercept any Spanish vessels on that route; the other half, under Burrough, would stay off the coast of Spain to stop any shipping that arrived by way of the African coast. Ralegh then returned to Plymouth on May 18.

Sir Walter's reluctance to return may have been occasioned by his fear that he might be seized and imprisoned. He had not only disobeyed the queen by refusing to return immediately, but he also knew that the court was now rife with the news of his long-hidden marriage to Elizabeth Throckmorton—or at least the fact that she was pregnant and he was responsible. But with characteristic courage, Ralegh returned not to Sherborne but to Durham House, where he awaited a summons to appear at court. For some reason, Elizabeth took no action for more than six weeks. Then suddenly, without warning, both Sir Walter and Lady Ralegh were seized and put into separate quarters in the Tower of London. There Ralegh was in despair. He had not been charged with any crime, so there was no defense. If his marriage was the cause, it could not be denied. To him and to his lady, the situation appeared hopeless.

But for once Sir Walter's privateering got him released from his "depth of all misery." His actions against the Spanish bore fruit: Burrough, off the Spanish coast, captured a number of prizes, one of which, the *Madre de Dios,* was one of the largest and richest ships ever to be seized. This huge Portuguese carrack was a seven-decker of 1,600 tons, a crew of nearly 700, and a cargo rich beyond belief. Although estimates of its value vary widely (inflated or deflated according to the purpose of the assayer), one apparently authentic account gave the list of its East Indies cargo as

537 tons of spices, 8500 hundredweight of pepper, 900 hundredweight of cloves, 700 hundredweight of cinnamon, 500 hundredweight of cochineal, 59 hundredweight of mace, 59 hundredweight of nutmeg, 50 hundredweight of benjamin, 15 tons of ebony, two great crosses and another large piece of jewelry studded with diamonds, [and] chests overflowing with musk, pearls, amber, calicoes, drugs, silks, ivory, tapestries, silver, and gold. . . .

This was a king's (or rather queen's) ransom; an official estimate of its value placed it at £141,000, which in modern terms would be several millions of dollars. Nothing like it had ever been seen in England before—certainly not in Dartmouth, to which it was brought on September 8.

The temptation was too great; immediately, looting began. English seamen who believed that they deserved their portion could not wait and began removing cargo; others who came to view the ship ended by filling their pockets. The great wealth began slowly to ooze away. No one had the strength or authority to stop the thievery. John Hawkins wrote frantically to Lord Burghley that special action was vital, and it was his belief that the only one who would handle the situation was the ship's owner, Ralegh. "Sir Walter Ralegh is the especial man," he wrote, and if Sir Walter were released, "it might very much set forth Her Majesty's service, and might benefit her portion." Burghley sent his son, Robert Cecil, down to survey the situation, and, surprisingly, Robert confirmed Hawkins's judgment that the situation was desperate and that Ralegh might be helpful.

Elizabeth, horrified at the thought of losing some of her share of the loot, ordered Ralegh's immediate release from the Tower—although Sir Walter was to remain in the custody of Sir Christopher Blount, an experienced military officer. Ralegh, naturally anxious to save his own huge investment, hurried to Dartmouth. His arrival was recorded by young Robert Cecil:

Within one half hour, Sir Walter Ralegh arrived with his keeper, Mr. Blount. I assure you, Sir, his poor servants, to the number of one hundred and forty goodly men, and all the mariners, came to him with such shouts and joy, as I never saw a man more troubled to quiet them in my life. But his heart is broken; for he is very extremely pensive longer than he is busied, in which he can toil terribly. The meeting between him and Sir John Gilbert was with tears on Sir John's part. Whensoever he is saluted with congratulations for liberty, he doth answer, 'No; I am still the Queen of England's poor captive.'

By his own popularity and powers of persuasion, Ralegh succeeded where others had failed: he not only stopped the looting but he also retrieved most of the stolen goods and saved the major portion of the cargo for distribution to the proper investors. Only he himself suffered. Perhaps he was buying his freedom, but the final distribution was eminently unfair. The queen took more than half for herself (£80,000) and gave a quarter (£40,000) to her current favorite, George Clifford, earl of Cumberland, a naval officer and courtier. Ralegh was given £24,000—much less than he had invested. But beyond this, Elizabeth granted him his freedom and his wife's freedom—but not her favor. Although the Raleghs were still not welcome at court, they were free to take up residence in Sherborne and again adopt the lives of West Country gentlefolk.

It was during this period of rustication that Ralegh began to consider alternate means of regaining the esteem and affection of the queen and nation and his place in court. Obviously, to redeem his favor, he needed to lay great gifts at the feet of the monarch. His ideas concerning a colonial empire had not succeeded; his forays on the oceans had produced only partially favorable results; something even more dramatic was required to meet his present needs.

The huge caches of precious metals and jewels returned by the

Spanish explorers Hernando Cortes and Francisco Pizzaro had been emptied. But had all the treasure cities of the western world been located and sacked? Both rumor and tradition suggested that they had not. Gossip had it that some of the Inca and Aztec rulers had escaped the Spanish, taking with them vast stores of golden idols and treasures. Others spoke of undiscovered civilizations buried in the reaches of South America not yet visited by Europeans. Tales of a lost empire of the Incas, El Dorado, the city of gold, where an Indian king and his followers retained fabulous wealth and covered themselves with gold dust, had attracted followers, just as the tales of Atlantis and Cathay had done. It was almost inevitable that in dreaming his great dreams, Ralegh would turn to tales like these.

This was the golden opportunity Ralegh sought. Once he had conceived his great plan, nothing would satisfy him but discovering this lost city and laying its treasures at the feet of the queen. And (as his dreams grew) he might establish for Elizabeth a new colony in the northern South American region of Guiana—not a colony of imported settlers living in a hostile environment but one of native Indians who had been converted to English religion, English social customs, and English citizenship and who would in effect serve as local defenders of Englishmen and English trade against their Spanish enemies. Guiana would be a rich colony under the benevolent rule of Queen Elizabeth—Ralegh's gift to the world's preeminent monarch.

XIX. Preparation for Guiana, 1595

Once Ralegh had conceived his plan for founding a golden empire in Guiana, he began to implement his dream. Richard Hakluyt was assigned the task of collecting all known documents about the land and its fabled cities; Thomas Harriot was to seek out rutters, charts, and maps of the South America then known and to concentrate on the region of the Orinoco and Amazon rivers, long assumed to be the gateways to the inner land where Manoa and the fabled city of El Dorado lay. Ralegh himself interviewed seamen who had ventured into the enemy-controlled waters around their deltas. Once more he followed his former practice of sending out a reconnaissance voyage— this time under the command of his most trusted captain, Jacob Whiddon—to obtain firsthand information about appropriate routes and to assess the strength and locations of the occupying Spanish forces.

Harriot was once more assigned the task of improving the navigational skills of Ralegh's seamen, as he had done before the Virginia voyages a decade earlier. A reference library with books and maps to be studied by the expedition's leaders was established at Durham House, and the scientific lectures from Harriot's *Arcticon,* a long-lost volume on the art of navigation, were revised and improved, as were the navigational instruments especially designed for each participating master. Harriot's rough notes for these lectures still exist; they show that even Sir Walter himself and his experienced Captain Whiddon, interested in bringing the last word of science to their sailing skills, were in attendance. Among Harriot's notes is an interesting bit of doggerel, hardly up to the standards of Elizabethan poetry but showing the linkage between his science and the possible success of the Guiana search for gold. Probably used as the close of his final lecture, Harriot's attempt to harness the muse reads as follows:

> Three new marriages here are made:
> One of the staff and sea astrolabe;
> Of the sun and star is another

Which now agree like sister and brother;
And chart and compass which now at bate [battle]
Will now agree like master and mate.
If you use them well in this your journey
They will be the King of Spain's attorney;
To bring you to silver and Indian gold,
Which will keep you in age from hunger and cold.
God speed you well, and send you fair weather
And that again we may meet together.

Although a few of Ralegh's friends shared his optimism about his returning laden with gold, many who had been supportive of him in the past were less sanguine. From his position as a Devonshire gentleman with little influence at court, Ralegh found support more difficult to obtain than it had earlier been. And the situation was made worse by the rumors that were beginning to circulate. Ralegh's integrity was under attack, and his liberal beliefs were raising questions about his orthodoxy. In 1592 a Catholic polemicist, knowing that Sir Walter had ambitions for a seat on the Privy Council, wrote a scathing attack on Elizabethan politicians, in which he accused Ralegh of going far beyond a rational skepticism and even of maintaining a "school of atheism." Although the charges may seem trivial to a modern reader, they were taken seriously by the devout Anglicans of that period.

During these years the English church was very rigorous in its attempts to root out Catholicism or any laxity of belief. Church attendance and close adherence to Anglican doctrine were required by law, and any infringement was subject to investigation. As a result of these rumors, there was formed a Commission in Causes Ecclesiastical, which established a special committee to look into any religious deviancy that might exist in Devon. This committee met at Cerne Abbas in March, 1594, and conducted hearings. Clergymen and other citizens were asked what they knew, had heard, or suspected was going on that might undermine the official religion. Extant records of these investigations clearly show that the major thrust of the questioning had to do with any possible "atheism" (a vague term in those days) or unorthodoxy in the speeches or actions of the Raleghs—Walter and Carew—Thomas Harriot, and Thomas Allen, a friend of Sir Walter who was under his command as lieutenant of Portland Castle. Nothing tangible came of these inquiries and no conclusions were reached, but the smoke they raised undoubtedly put Ralegh and his associates in a position in which all their actions remained suspect.

Yet in spite of these difficulties, Ralegh persevered. Although the queen was not personally interested in Guiana and was unwilling to invest any of her funds in the project, she did agree to issue to Sir Walter a patent giving him authority to discover and conquer lands unpossessed by any Christian king and going so far as to authorize him to "offend and enfeeble the King of Spain" as well—a license for privateering, thievery, or hostile acts that must have cheered Ralegh's heart. Lord High Admiral Charles Howard again came to Ralegh's aid, offering him his ship, the *Lion's Whelp,* under command of Captain George Gifford. Lord Cecil, one of the few government officials interested in Guiana, assisted with provisions. Two privateers were interested in getting under the protection of Ralegh's charter: Captains Amyas Preston and George Somer said they would go, although they did not show up at sailing time. Two others, Sir Robert Dudley and George Popham, indicated they would meet Ralegh at Trinidad but left there before he arrived. The core of the fleet Ralegh finally was able to raise consisted only of the *Lion's Whelp* under Gifford, Ralegh's own ship (nowhere named, but probably the *Bark Ralegh* or the *Roebuck*), commanded by Jacob Whiddon, and a small galley led by Lawrence Keymis, an Oxford fellow skilled in navigation, geography, and mathematics, who became one of Ralegh's most devoted followers for the rest of his life.

This was not a large expedition; it consisted only of the necessary seamen and approximately one hundred officers, gentlemen, and adventurers. Yet, it must have taxed Ralegh's resources at a time when his financial position was poor. There is no question but that he stretched his credit to the limit and made extreme demands on his friends and relatives for their support. The London merchants who had invested in Virginia were loath to provide funds for a voyage so largely exploratory. Only Ralegh's relative William Sanderson, a London merchant, was willing to raise funds and stand surety for his huge loans. A later lawsuit between the two men reveals that Sanderson "at the request and for the good of the said Sir Walter Ralegh and for his credit stood bound and engaged by him by bonds, money disbursed, and otherwise to the value of fifty thousand pounds and upward at one instant of time when the credit of the said Sir Walter Ralegh in itself could not otherwise attain thereunto."

Far from being grateful, according to Sanderson, Ralegh tricked him. At midnight on the night he sailed, while bidding goodbye to his wife and friends and under the pretext of examining the accounts,

Ralegh seized the accounts and gave them to Harriot, thus leaving Sanderson with no record of his contributions or any means of collecting on the obligations he had incurred in Ralegh's behalf. Whether these charges were true or false is not known, but the evidence makes it clear that in order to finance his voyage to Guiana, Ralegh had not only contributed what resources he could raise but also became indebted for the princely sum of £50,000.

XX. The First Guiana Voyage

Early in the morning of February 6, 1595, the four ships, long delayed by adverse winds, set sail on what for Ralegh must have been his great adventure. They took the customary route—south to the Canaries and then due west to the West Indies. Again, contrary winds separated the voyagers: Ralegh and Sir Robert Crosse, an old comrade who had fought beside Ralegh in Cadiz harbor, arrived first, but no sign of the vessels of Gifford or Keymis could be found. After taking aboard fresh water, wine, and provisions and waiting a week for the bark and galley, Ralegh made the decision to sail on without them. A swift crossing under favorable conditions brought them on March 22 to Trinidad, where they cast anchor off the southwest shore. Once more Sir Walter waited several days for Cross and Keymis and then moved on to the vicinity of present-day Port of Spain to chart the shores, rivers, and physical features of the area. During this time no person—native or Spanish—was seen.

According to Ralegh's account, it was at Port of Spain that he first had contact with the Spanish, as some of them came aboard "to buy linen of the company." With characteristic guile, Sir Walter wined and dined them on board his flagship and plied the Spanish with questions about Guiana,

by means whereof I learned of one and another as much of the estate of Guiana as I could or as they knew, for those poor soldiers having been many years without wine, a few draughts made them merry, in which mood they vaunted of Guiana and of the riches thereof and all they knew of the ways and passages. . . .

To mislead his befuddled guests, he pretended his visit was solely "for the relief of those English which I had planted in Virginia, whereof the bruit was come among them," which (he added in an aside) "I had performed on my return if extremity of weather had not forced me from the said coast."

Ralegh had a dual purpose in questioning the Spaniards: to save him from needless difficulty, he wanted information about the country and its peoples; and he also wanted to avenge the treachery shown by his Spanish rival, Antonio de Berrio, to Captain Jacob Whiddon during the latter's visit there the previous year, when Berrio invited some of Whiddon's men ashore and then murdered them.

Ralegh well knew the Spanish leader he was up against. He described Berrio, who, then at the ripe age of sixty, had devoted his last years and fortune to the search for El Dorado, as "well descended . . . very valiant and liberal, and a gentleman of great assuredness and of a great heart." Berrio had first reached the Orinoco from Central America, entering the upper reaches of the river in 1584 and sailing down it from its source. There, on the island of Trinidad, opposite the Orinoco delta, he had established his major base of operations. From this base he had continued his exploration of the river and its environs year after year, covering more of the territory than any white man had ever done before. Berrio's exploits had so impressed his king that Philip had granted him a royal commission as governor of El Dorado. Ralegh knew that if he were to succeed, he must first learn "of the enterprises of Berrio, by what means or fault he failed [to find the city of gold], and how he meant to prosecute the same."

To this end, Ralegh rounded up all the Indian chiefs he could find on Trinidad and questioned them in detail about the Spaniards. According to his later account (which may have been exaggerated to serve his own ends), they told him of Spanish mistreatment, even atrocities, saying that Berrio had made slaves of the natives, had "kept them in chains, and dropped their naked bodies with burning bacon, and other such torments." They convinced Ralegh that his instincts were sound—that he could make friends with the native chiefs, ally them to his cause, and unify their diverse tribes in common purpose to accept English government and reject and fight the Spanish as invaders.

But as a soldier accustomed to treacherous warfare, sneak attacks, and ambushes, Ralegh saw that he must first protect his forces for their voyage up the Orinoco. As he wrote:

considering that to enter Guiana by small boats, to depart 400 or 500 miles from my ships and to leave a garrison at my back interested in the same enterprise (who also expected daily supplies out of Spain), I should have savored much of the ass. . . .

So Ralegh attacked. At dusk, when visibility was poorest, his men attacked the Spanish guards of Berrio's stronghold, overcame them, and put them to the sword. He then divided his 100 soldiers into two forces: Captain Thomas Caulfeilde with sixty formed the vanguard;

Sir Walter with forty remained in the rear for support. They marched all night and just before daybreak launched their attack on the new city—S. Joseph de Oruna—that Berrio had built for his headquarters. Spanish accounts tell of a heroic defense, but Ralegh was not so kind: "They abode not any fight after a few shot," he declared, as they captured Berrio, routed his forces, burned the city, and carried prisoners back to their ships for questioning. Later that same day, by good chance, the long-overdue ships of Ralegh's expedition arrived to assist in the celebrations of victory. Reinforcement and additional supplies at hand, Sir Walter was ready for his move toward the city of gold.

This engraving depicts Sir Walter Ralegh and members of his South American expedition laying waste a Spanish settlement in Guiana and capturing a group of Spanish soldiers. Engraving from Theodor de Bry's *America,* Part 7 (1599), original copy in North Carolina Collection.

How seriously Ralegh took the information he obtained from the captured Berrio is difficult to assess. But from his own account, his information concerning geographical features, natives, and tribal chiefs appears to have been accurate. But Berrio also lent credence to the fabulous tales that had so intrigued Ralegh and caused so many of his countrymen to question his veracity. Sir Walter solemnly recited Berrio's belief in the tale of the Golden Man of El Dorado:

. . . at the times of their solemn feasts, when the emperor carouses with his captains, tributories, and governors, the manner is thus. All those that pledge him are first stripped naked, and their bodies anointed all over with a kind of white Balsam. . . . When they are anointed all over, certain servants of the Emperor, having prepared gold made into a fine powder, blow it through hollow canes upon their naked bodies, until they be all shining from the foot to the head. . . .

Much more immediately appealing to Ralegh were Berrio's stories of the natives' "images of gold in their temples, the plates, armors, and shield of gold which they use in their wars."

Berrio also convinced Sir Walter that there really existed a nation of women warriors (fabulous since classical times as the Amazons) who gave the river their name. Ralegh admitted that he was

very desirous to understand the truth of those warlike women, because of some it is believed, of others not. And though I digress from my purpose, yet I will set down what has been delivered as truth of those women. . . . The nations of these women are on the south side of the river in the provinces of Topago, and their chiefest strengths and retreats are in the islands situate on the south side of the entrance, some sixty leagues within the mouth of the said river. . . . But they which are not far from Guiana do accompany with men but once a year, and for the time of one month, which I gather by their relation to be in April. At that time all the Kings of the border do assemble with the Queens of the Amazons, and after the Queens have chosen [their mates], the rest cast lots for their Valentines. This one month they feast, dance, and drink of their wines in abundance, and the Moon being done, they all depart to their own provinces. If they conceive and be delivered of a son, they return him to the father; if of a daughter, they nourish it and retain it, and as many as have daughters send unto their begetters a present, all being desirous to increase their own sex and kind, but that they cut off the right dug of the breast, I do not find to be true. It was further told me that in the wars they took prisoners . . . in the end for certain they put them to death, for they are said to be very cruel and bloodthirsty.

Another group of fabulous natives that intrigued Ralegh was the "nation of inhumane Cannibals which inhabit the rivers of Guanipa and Berreese." The English had already known man-eating cannibals in the tribe of Caribs they had encountered in Santo Domingo. But these were more astounding: "They are called 'Ewaipanoma'; they are reported to have their eyes in their shoulders and their mouths in the middle of their breasts, and that a long train of hair grows backward between their shoulders." Such tales had been around for generations, but Ralegh reinstated them to popularity in England;

86

and it was undoubtedly his account that led Shakespeare to have Othello speak of

> the Cannibals that each other eat,
> The Anthropophagi, and men whose heads
> Do grow beneath their shoulders.

Ralegh was ready for action. Strange lands, unknown natives, bizarre customs, fabulous creatures—not to mention the gold of the lost Inca tribes—all these were ahead of him, and he could not hide his eagerness from his men, or even from Berrio. Confessing his true purposes in his voyage up the river, Ralegh released his prisoners, called his leaders into conference, and prepared to enter the unknown reaches of the Orinoco.

XXI. Up the Orinoco

Having learned from Berrio all he could, Ralegh was ready for his first real exploration of the New World. But his initial excitement was cooled somewhat at the outset when his pilots could not locate the deep channel in the delta that Jacob Whiddon had found the year before. The pilots learned from friendly natives that cannibal tribes were hunting with poisoned arrows, so they were forced to stay far away from the banks of the twisted maze of waterways that made up the entrance to the main stream. A captured Arawak agreed to guide them, but, Ralegh observed, "of that which he entered he was utterly ignorant, for he had not seen it in twelve years before, when he was young and of no judgment." For a time it seemed as if they were totally lost: "if God had not sent us another help, we might have wandered a whole year in that labyrinth of rivers ere we had found any way either out or in." That help came in the form of a friendly, old, and experienced native who was able and willing to take them to the main stream. Ralegh was impressed by the local tribe:

These Tivitivas are a very goodly people and very valiant, and have the most manly speech and most deliberate that ever I heard. . . . In the summer they have houses on the ground as in other places: in the winter they dwell upon the trees, where they build very artificial towns and villages . . . for between May and September the river of Orinoco rises thirty feet upright. . . . They refuse to feed of ought but that which nature without labor bringeth forth.

But although the natives could survive from the bounty of the land, Sir Walter and his party found themselves in trouble. The heat, the humidity, and the strenuous exertion required in rowing against the current every foot of the way were taking their toll. As Ralegh explained:

In the bottom of an old Gallego which I caused to be fashioned like a Galley, and in one barge, two wherries, and a ship's boat of the "Lion's Whelp," we carried 100 persons and their victuals for a month . . . being all driven to lie in the rain and weather, in the open air, in the burning sun, and upon the hard boards, and to dress our meat, and to carry all manner of furniture in them, wherewith they were so pestered and unsavory, that what with victuals being mostly fish, with the wet clothes of so many men thrust together and the heat of the sun, I will undertake that there was never any prison in England that could be found more unsavory and loathsome, especially for myself, who had for many years before been dieted and cared for in a sort far differing.

Things were so bad that Sir Walter considered hanging the pilot, and refrained only because the man's knowledge was essential for their further progress. Just as things seemed the worst, however, they reached the main stream of the river, where, after their long stay in the delta swamps, they found its fertile higher banks impressive. Ralegh was as enthusiastic as his Virginia settlers had been at their first view of their new homeland:

On both sides of this river, we passed the most beautiful country that ever mine eyes beheld: and whereas all that we had seen before was nothing but woods, prickles, bushes, and thorns, here we beheld plains of twenty miles in length, the grass short and green, and in divers parts groves of trees by themselves, as if they had been by all the art and labor in the world so made of purpose; and still as we rowed, the deer came down feeding by the river's side, as if they had been used to a keeper's call.

Yet even there, danger lurked. The river harbored "those ugly serpents," the alligators, which the people called lagartos. So many thousands of them were there that the Orinoco was locally named "the river of Lagartos." The dangerous nature of the reptiles was brought home to the Englishmen quickly as "a Negro, a very proper young fellow, that leaping out of the Galley to swim in the mouth of this river, was in all our sights taken and devoured with one of those Lagartos."

Following this tragedy, the party continued rowing upstream on the huge river, which the natives insisted extended a full thousand miles to the west. As they proceeded, Ralegh, in addition to charting the river's course and seeking information about El Dorado, took pains to seek out and befriend the native chiefs, or casiques, as they were called. This was rendered difficult because the Indians, fearing the cruelties they associated with the Spanish, fled from all white men. But Sir Walter persisted in his goal to impress them with the friendliness of the English, to win them to the queen, and to make

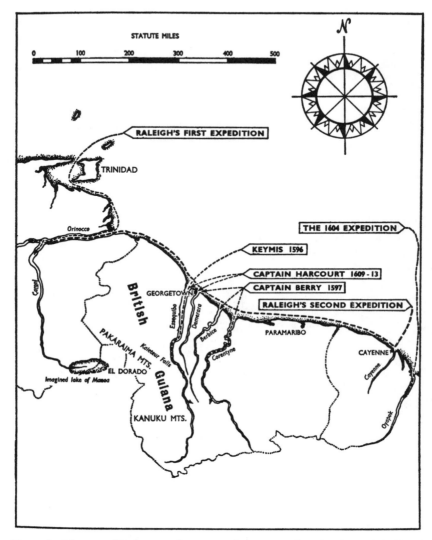

Shown in this map of Guiana are the routes of voyages undertaken by various English explorers in the late sixteenth and early seventeenth centuries. Map from Henry Clapp, *With Raleigh to British Guiana* (London: Frederick Muller, Ltd., 1965), p. 13.

them allies against the Spanish. The casiques were doubtful, for the Spanish had convinced them

that we [the English] were men eaters and Cannibals: but when the poor men and women had seen us, and that we gave them meat . . . they began to conceive the deceit and purpose of the Spaniards, who indeed (as they confessed) took from them their wives and daughters daily, and used them for the satisfying of their own lusts. . . .

According to Ralegh's account, with respect to the matter of the abuse of women, at least, the English were true to their vows to the Virgin Queen and did not molest the native women. This behavior won friends among the Indians, who were accustomed to brutal treatment by the Spanish.

How Ralegh and his party met the native chiefs is best illustrated by his detailed account of his first encounter with Topiawari, whom Sir Walter called "the proudest and wisest of all the Orinoqueponi." By this time, they had rowed their small fleet several hundred miles inland and were approaching the area near the promised entrance to the land of gold. As Ralegh tells the story:

The next day we arrived at the port of Morequito and anchored there, sending away one of our pilots to seek the King of Aromaia, uncle to More-quito, slain by Berrio. . . . The next day following, before noon he came to us on foot from his house, which was 14 English miles (himself being 110 years old), and returned on foot the same day, and with him many of the borderers, with many women and children, that came to wonder at our na-tion, and to bring us down victuals, which they did with great plenty, as venison, pork, hens, chickens, foul, fish, with divers sorts of excellent fruits, and roots, and great abundance of Pinas [pineapples], the princess of fruits, that grow under the sun, especially those of Guiana. They brought us also store of bread, and their wine, and a sort of Parakeet, no bigger than wrens, and of all other sorts both small and great. One of them gave me a beast called by the Spaniards Armadilla, which they call Cassacam, which seems to be all barred over with small plates . . . with a white horn growing in his hinder parts, as big as a great hunting horn, which they used to wind in-stead of a trumpet. . . .

After this old king had rested a while in a little tent that I caused to be set up, I began by my interpreter to discourse with him of the death of More-quito, his predecessor, and afterwards of the Spaniards. And before I went any farther I made him know the cause of my coming thither, whose ser-vant I was, and that the Queen's pleasure was [that] I should undertake the voyage for their defense and to deliver them from the tyranny of the Spaniards, dilating at large (as I had done before to those of Trinidad) [on]

Her Majesty's greatness, Her justice, Her charity to all nations, with as many of the rest of her beauties and virtues as either I could express or they conceive, all which being with great admiration attentively heard.

Topiawari was impressed by Ralegh's presentation: he offered full support for his expedition, said that he would willingly serve such a gracious monarch, and indicated that he would help recruit other chiefs to the cause. He gave Ralegh a great deal of information about the area of the upper reaches of the Orinoco and the tribes he would encounter. In return, Ralegh promised that this was but a preliminary journey and that he would return the following year with an armed fleet and enough soldiers to overwhelm all the Spanish forces in Guiana.

Following their meeting with Topiawari, the party proceeded upstream, seeking the place where the Caroni River entered the Orinoco, a point that had become their goal. Ralegh had been convinced from his reading, reinforced by his questioning of Berrio and Topiawari, that it was the Caroni River that would provide access to the lake and city of Manoa. When they arrived, they were unprepared for the roar of its rapids. "We heard the great roar and fall of the river," Sir Walter reported, "but when we came to enter with our barge and wherries, thinking to have gone up some forty miles to the nations of the Cassipagotos, we were not able with a barge of eight oars to row one stone's cast in an hour," although the river was as broad as the Thames. This was disappointing. Although they tried both sides and the center of the river, they could make no headway. Finally they were forced to seek the shore and send for the local chiefs to come to them.

Conference with the casiques who responded to his call reinforced the information old Topiawari had given Ralegh: that the tribes of the Caroni were enemies of a lost Inca tribe that dwelt nearby. The casiques reinforced Berrio's tales of a great silver mine so rich that almost pure ore lay on the surface of a mountain a short distance from the river. They also spoke of the awesome falls of the Caroni, some twenty miles upstream, near which nuggets of pure gold and silver might be picked up from the riverbed. Hearing these reports, Sir Walter split his party: his nephew John Gilbert and his cousin Butshead Gorges were to take thirty soldiers and go overland to a village where they could obtain guides to the mountain mine on the borders of El Dorado; a second group, led by Captain Whiddon and protected by eight soldiers, was to proceed to the falls to search the riverbed for ore to take back to England; a third party, headed by Ralegh, was to visit the head of the great falls, there to survey the surrounding plains and to look for signs of the area surrounding Lake Manoa.

This was the point of Ralegh's farthest advance into the South American continent, and, according to his account, his most emotional experience. He was almost lyrical in his description:

When we ran to the tops of the first hills of the plains adjoining to the river, we beheld that wonderful breach of waters which ran down Caroni; and might from that mountain see the river, how it ran in three parts above twenty miles off, and there appeared some ten or twelve overfalls in sight, every one as high over the other as a church tower, which fell with that fury that the rebound of waters made it seem as if it had all been covered over with a great shower or rain: and in some places we took it at the first for a smoke that had risen over some great town. For mine own part, I was well persuaded from thence to have returned, being a very ill footman, but the rest were all so desirous to go near the said strange thunder of waters as they drew me on by little and little till we came into the next valley where we might better discern the same. I never saw a more beautiful country,

During Ralegh's first Guiana voyage (1595) he and his men entered the Orinoco River and met a number of native Indian chiefs on friendly terms. Sir Walter was particularly impressed with an elderly chief named Topiawari and with the abundance of foodstuffs and fauna in the area. Engraving from de Bry's *America,* Part 7; original copy in North Carolina Collection.

nor more lively prospects, hill so raised here and there over the valley, the river winding into divers branches, the plains adjoining without bush or stubble, all fair green grass, the ground of hard sand easy to march on, either for horse or foot, the deer crossing in every path, the birds towards the evening singing on every tree with a thousand several tunes, cranes and herons of white, crimson, and carnation perching on the river's side, the air fresh with a gentle easterly wind, and every stone that we stooped to pick up promising either gold or silver by its complexion.

Glorious though this experience was, it was time to return. The rainy season with its discomforts had begun, Berrio's reinforcements were due, and it was wise to stay no longer. The boats turned and started downstream. The passage was naturally easier than the upstream voyage had been; with the river's current helping rather than hindering, Ralegh estimated that nearly 100 miles could be covered in a day. Just one day after leaving the mouth of the Caroni, the party arrived at Morequito, having covered a distance that had taken more than a week on the upstream journey. There they anchored once more, since Ralegh, impressed by Topiawari, wanted another conference with him before they departed.

During their second meeting, they formulated plans for further action. Topiawari, feeling the urgency of his age, was anxious to proceed: he wanted Ralegh to leave him fifty soldiers to begin their campaign to unite the natives for the queen and against the Spanish. This Ralegh recognized was not feasible. But he did pledge to return and meanwhile "resolved Topiawari [as] Lord of Aromaia," naming him his personal deputy in his absence. On his part, Topiawari placed in Ralegh's custody his only son and heir, who was to accompany Sir Walter on his return to England and serve as intermediary between the two men as they planned future strategies. In turn, Ralegh left with Topiawari two Englishmen. Francis Sparrow, a servant to Captain Gifford, and like John White an artist, desired to remain behind in order "to describe the country with his pen." Hugh Goodwin, a boy servant to Ralegh who had proved facile with languages, also remained to learn the tribal languages and prepare himself to serve as translator on Sir Walter's return.[6]

Although Sir Walter later put the best possible face on his voyage of "discovery," he must have been discouraged on his return to Trinidad. Nowhere had he found any tangible evidence of a city of gold or any golden idols or plates that he could take back as evidence of the wealth of the land. All he had were a few samples of ore picked up near the Caroni and some other samples Keymis said came from a mysterious mountain mine. Certainly, the English backers of his expedition would expect more than this if they were to underwrite later voyages. With typical resourcefulness, Ralegh decided to take advantage of his patent right to privateer by plundering the towns of the Spanish Main, as Drake had done earlier. In this, too, he was disappointed. Although he later claimed to have taken ransom and loot from Margarita, St. Mary's, Cumana, and Rio de la Hacha, these claims are denied by Spanish records. St. Mary's and Rio de la Hacha refused to pay Ralegh's demands for ransom, so Sir Walter's men partially burned the towns. Cumana apparently was even worse: there Ralegh's troops were repulsed by the Spanish, and he lost a Grenville cousin and Captain Caulfeilde. Jacob Whiddon, his friend and trusted companion, he buried on Trinidad. And as a last rebuff, when he attempted to ransom Berrio and Captain Alvaro Jorge at Margarita for 1,400 ducats, the governor refused to pay on the ground that the English had not met their own conditions. Sir Walter finally was obliged to free Berrio without receiving any compensation.

Even Ralegh's hope to visit the Virginia colony on his return was denied him. On July 13, 1595, his small fleet made rendezvous with Captains Amyas Preston and George Somers, who were searching for Spanish prizes. They sailed together for a time without success, then Ralegh turned northward for Virginia. But by that time the weather was bad and the winds were not propitious. The fleet was forced to turn back to England, where it arrived in August, six months after its departure.

XXII. Guiana: The Aftermath

Ralegh's return to England was as unpleasant as he had feared. Lord Cecil was disgusted: his large investment had returned only a few samples of ore of dubious quality. Although gold assays made by Ralegh showed the ore to be rich, independent analyses by an official of the mint declared them worthless. One rumor around London was that the ore had not been collected in Guiana but had instead been brought from Barbary and taken to Guiana by Sir Walter to be found there. Another rumor went so far as to declare that Ralegh himself had not gone to the Orinoco but had instead hidden out in Cornwall and only pretended to leave the country.

Ralegh naturally was incensed. Within a very short time he produced his own account of his expedition, *The Discoverie of the Large, Rich, and Bewtiful Empyre of Guiana, with a Relation of the Great and Golden Citie of Manoa,* which he dedicated to two of his major investors—Sir Robert Cecil and Sir Charles Howard. Sir Walter's account was clear and graphic, giving details of the nature of the country and its inhabitants that Englishmen had never heard, and was so widely read that it went through two editions in 1596. However, although it stimulated much interest, it did nothing to enlist support for additional voyages.

Nevertheless, Ralegh continued to hope for financial support; and he took seriously his pledge to Topiawari and the other casiques to return with naval and military support. But first, he realized, he needed to locate the channel through the shallow delta, which would accommodate ships of greater draft. Thus, he continued to invest his own resources in Guiana. Harriot was given the task of revising all the maps with information gleaned in 1595; Keymis was to make a voyage for further exploration of the Orinoco delta, with instructions to reach the rich mountain mine they had been forced to bypass the previous year. Before the end of January, 1596, Keymis had completed his preparations and, in the *Darling of London,* followed by the pinnace *Discovery,* set sail on this new mission.

On his return, Keymis, as Ralegh had done, wrote the most persuasive account of his expedition possible, *A Relation of the Second*

THE
DISCOVERIE
OF THE LARGE,
RICH, AND BEVVTIFVL
EMPYRE OF GVIANA, WITH

a relation of the great and Golden Citie
of Manoa *(which the Spanyards call* El
Dorado) And of the Prouinces of *Emeria,*
Artomaia, Amapaia , and other Countries, with their riuers, ad-
ioyning.

Performed in the yeare 1 5 9 5. by Sir
W. Ralegh Knight , Captaine of her
Maiesties Guard, Lo. Warden
of the Stanneries , and her High-
nesse Lieutenant generall
of the Countie of
Cornewall.

Imprinted at London by Robert Robinson.
1 5 9 6.

In order to counteract rumors in London that he had not actually taken part in the 1595 voyage to Guiana, Sir Walter published the following year *The Discoverie of the Large, Rich, and Bewtiful Empyre of Guiana, with a Relation of the Great and Golden Citie of Manoa,* his own account of the expedition. The title page of the work is shown above. From an original copy in the North Carolina Collection.

Voyage to Guiana, Performed and Written in the year 1596 by Lawrence Keymis, Gent.; the book was dedicated to Sir Walter. On this second voyage, too, the ocean crossing had been made in foul weather; the pinnace did not arrive at all, and it was mid-March before the *Darling* reached the coast of Guiana. For twenty-three days Keymis and his crew cruised along the delta, charting the coast and entrances and seeking a deep-channel entrance. On April 6 they discovered a channel through which Keymis was able to sail his ship directly into the main stream of the Orinoco. All along the way, he reported, the natives rushed to greet them, thinking them the reinforcements promised by Ralegh to defeat their Spanish enemies.

From two casiques—Anawra and Aparwa—Keymis was informed of developments during the past year. Old Topiawari had died, and his only son (now christened Gualtero, after Sir Walter) would be king on his return from England. In his absence, the tribes had dispersed to escape Spanish persecution. But in the meantime the Spanish had overrun the entire area surrounding the Caroni River. Berrio's son had arrived with reinforcements—not only more soldiers, but also 600 colonists to establish permanent communities along the river and 60 Negro slaves to work the silver mines.

With fresh water and provisions, Keymis sailed the *Darling* up the river—a much easier passage than that accomplished by rowing. In just eight days of easy sailing he arrived at the Port of Topiawari prepared to make the trek to the inland mountain where the mine was reputed to be. But there he found his plans foiled. During the year, Berrio had erected a village just three miles east of the Caroni entrance; but even worse, he had built a fort and garrison at the mouth of the Caroni, effectively blocking entrance to what Berrio (as well as Ralegh and Keymis) believed to be the source of Inca gold. Unable to pursue this primary objective, Keymis was in a quandary. Although his pilot, John Gilbert, insisted that he could lead them to a hidden gold mine, the danger was great, since the proposed route took them between the Spanish troops and the unknown Arawak tribes nearby. Keymis refused to take the chance; he turned his ships downstream and in eight days brought the *Darling* to the open sea. There at long last he found the *Discovery* waiting, but in such bad shape that he had to burn it to prevent it from being taken by the Spanish. On its return voyage to England the party looked for Spanish prizes to seize or tobacco to purchase, but failed to find either and was forced to return with nothing to help defray the costs of the voyage.

Keymis's report to Ralegh of his failure to bring back ore or to locate the source of Inca gold sounded the death knell for Ralegh's hopes to establish a Guiana empire under his queen. Absolutely essential for his purpose was an armed force to support the native Indians in their war against the Spanish. Such military support required money—money that Elizabeth would not advance and, as had become apparent, could not be drawn from the wealth of the land itself.

Keymis did what he could to ease the situation. His *Relation* is both an apology to Ralegh for the failure of his voyage and a blatant attempt to win support from Elizabeth, Cecil, and other possible adventurers. It was a small matter, Keymis argued, that they had returned with little tangible gold. The very way in which the Spanish were defending the land gave evidence of the richness of the prize and their fear that the English would wrest it from them. But his fervent pleas, like Ralegh's, fell on deaf ears. The queen was more concerned about the massing of Spanish warships in the harbor of Cadiz than the tribulations of a few primitive Indians on the Orinoco. Sir Robert Cecil wanted more from his investment than political promises and a few barren rocks. And the London merchants found it more profitable to invest in raids on Spanish shipping—to steal the gold the Spanish had stolen from the Indians—than to go to the source to extract the wealth by hard labor. England was not ready for Sir Walter's dreams of empire. Although the day was close at hand, it was not to dawn under the aegis of the Virgin Queen.

XXIII. Fortune's Tennis Ball

The vagaries of fate that inspired Robert Naunton to compare Ralegh's fortunes to the ups and downs of a tennis ball continued during the two decades following Sir Walter's voyage to Guiana. Ralegh's "impossible" tales about El Dorado and his failure to return any Inca gold or silver brought him much derision and popular abuse. And yet, although he acknowledged that he had set out for Guiana "in the winter of my life" (he was forty-three years old at the time) and had returned "beggared and withered," Ralegh still clung to his hopes that he could once again restore his fortunes to their former high estate. To do so, he returned to his profession as a soldier.

England was still fearful of another invasion by Spain. Indeed, in November, 1595, three months after his return from Guiana, Ralegh wrote to Cecil and the Privy Council that the Spanish were gathering a huge fleet in the port of Cadiz in preparation for an invasion of Ireland. Ralegh feared danger to Devon and Cornwall, for which he was responsible. After interminable delays, Elizabeth at last agreed to send a battle squadron to Spain and a formidable English armada was assembled. Ninety-six armed ships augmented by twenty-four Dutch vessels were placed under the joint command of Lord High Admiral Howard and Elizabeth's fiery favorite, the earl of Essex. Ten thousand soldiers under Sir Francis Vere, commander of the English army in the Netherlands, were returned from the Low Countries to man the expedition. Planning was placed under a council of war that included Lord Howard; Sir Francis Vere; Conyers Clifford, a subordinate army officer; Ralegh; and Sir George Carew, Ralegh's cousin. In the final disposition of command the naval forces were divided into four squadrons, one of which was to be commanded by Ralegh.

In June, 1597, the flotilla moved to the attack. But in spite of long planning sessions, the fleet was badly organized and confused. Admiral Howard was old and cautious; Essex was excitable and reckless; Vere was jealous and demanding. Although he was the least experienced of the commanders, Ralegh emerged as a natural leader: it was he who presented the plans of attack when all disagreed; it was he who prevented Essex from landing his troops on the side of Cadiz, where their extinction was inevitable; and it was he in his new two-deck warship the *Warspite* who led the final assault on the great war galleons that had destroyed Grenville's *Revenge,* declaring that he was "resolved to be revenged for the *Revenge,* or to second her with mine own life."

The fight was short but bloody; the Spanish panicked at the last minute: two of the four major warships destroyed themselves, the other two capitulated. The inhabitants of Cadiz surrendered and offered ransom to their captors. The great prize, however—the huge Spanish merchant fleet being guarded by the warships—was set on fire by the Spanish and thus lost to the English commanders, who argued about ransom. The English fleet returned home with a tremendous victory but without the loot that would have paid the costs of the invasion.

The triumph at Cadiz received a mixed reaction in England. The people were jubilant and made Essex the hero of the hour. But Elizabeth was furious: in the joy of victory, Essex had knighted sixty-six of his followers (Howard had created only five knights following the Armada of 1588)—strictly against her orders. To punish him, she took nearly all of his share of ransom for herself. Ralegh, still not fully in favor, complained that his share was less than Vere's. He wrote: "What the Generals have gotten, I know least; they protest it is little. For my part I have gotten a lame leg, and a deformed.... I have possession of naught but poverty and pain."

But in reality Sir Walter received a good deal more. His bravery and judgment had earned the respect of both Sir Robert Cecil and Lord Burghley, and they insisted to the queen that it was Ralegh, not Essex, who was the hero at Cadiz. The queen was stubborn, but they persisted; and a year later, on July 1, 1597, Ralegh was taken back to court and restored to full favor for the first time since his disgrace six years earlier. Rowland White, a member of the court, wrote that Elizabeth received Sir Walter

very graciously, and gave him full authority to execute his place as Captain of the Guard, which immediately he undertook and swore many men into the places void. In the evening he rode abroad with the Queen and had private conference with her; and now he comes boldly to the privy-chamber as he was wont.

This was probably the happiest period in Ralegh's life since his early days at court.

With this renewed security, Sir Walter was again able to consider his colonial aspirations. There are suggestions that there may have been two attempts to reach the Virginia settlement before 1600, but details are lacking. It is known that Ralegh was seeking information about the colonists in 1601 and 1602. In 1602 he outfitted a small bark under the command of Samuel Mace for this purpose. Mace conferred with Harriot about the Indians, their language, and the types of trading supplies that he should take with him. Details of this trip are sparse, but during that year Mace apparently landed in the vicinity of Cape Fear (nearly 200 miles south of Roanoke) and spent almost a month trading with the Indians of the region. He returned with a valuable cargo of sassafras but with no news of the Lost Colony or its fate. The following year, 1603, Bartholomew Gilbert was sent out in the *Elizabeth* with specific instructions to search the Chesapeake Bay area for the colonists. By misadventure, he landed north of the bay, where, during an exploratory trip, he and a number of his men were killed by the natives. It was only with difficulty that the ship was able to return to London—without news of the settlers. In 1603 Mace was again sent out for information about the City of Ralegh colony and developments in Guiana, but no report of this voyage exists.

During Elizabeth's final years, Ralegh's role at court was changed. He was no longer the romantic favorite of the queen; that role was reserved for Essex. Ralegh had become an old friend, mature counsellor, and trusted adviser to the monarch. As a member of Parliament he had earned a reputation as a most convincing speaker, one who espoused the cause of the common citizens as well as the queen. Even in his dealings with Essex, who was growing wilder daily, he remained friendly, attempting to moderate the earl's arrogance and boundless ambition and acting as peacemaker in their personal disputes.

But ultimately, Ralegh's association with Essex began to work against him. Essex, in spite of his irrationality and final treason in attempting to wrest the crown from Elizabeth, was a popular figure and the idol of the masses. His execution in 1601 was a most unpopular act. As captain of the Queen's Guard, Ralegh was officially in attendance. At first he stood near the block to hear the last words of his friend and rival. But when the attending crowd showed resentment at this, he retired to the shelter of the armory, where he could fulfill his duties but not be visible to the crowd. But the populace did not forgive. They felt Ralegh was the villain of the piece and wrongly blamed him for having had a hand in the sentence of death for their idol. This judgment generated an antagonism that plagued him for the rest of his life.

Elizabeth never got over the loss of her arrogant, irrational, but charming favorite. She was suddenly an old woman, indecisive, unwilling to face problems, leaving affairs of state to her ministers. Nearly seventy, she was afraid to die. And, although she would leave the throne without an heir, she would not discuss the succession. As a result, all consideration of the future of the monarchy had to be done in complete secrecy. There was, as a result, much backstage maneuvering among her ministers and the political figures of the state. Ralegh remained aloof from these matters; he had been loyal to the queen, and he realized that she was solely responsible for his position and support. He, too, could not bear to think of her death. Others, however, were scheming to make capital of a new monarch.

Most active of the schemers was a man Ralegh considered a very close friend, Robert Cecil, the physically deformed son of Lord Burghley, who had succeeded his father as Elizabeth's principal minister. Although Cecil appeared friendly to Ralegh, history has shown that he used Machiavellian duplicity in his political dealings during Elizabeth's last years. Whenever Sir Walter's name was proposed as appointee to the Privy Council, Cecil privately opposed it. When the queen wanted to make Ralegh the earl of Pembroke, Cecil employed various ruses to stop the process. When private negotiations were made with James VI of Scotland to succeed Elizabeth on

Robert Cecil, believed by Ralegh to be a close friend, schemed against Sir Walter during Elizabeth's last years on the throne. He likewise influenced Elizabeth's successor, James VI of Scotland, against Ralegh. Engraving from Lodge, *Portraits of Illustrious Personages*, IV.

the English throne, Cecil built his own image as a shrewd counsellor by warning James against hidden enemies of the court, foremost of whom, he alleged, were Ralegh and his friends Henry Brooke, Lord Cobham, and Henry Percy, earl of Northumberland. And when James asked for details, Cecil sent Ralegh's most venemous enemy, Henry Howard, earl of Northampton, to poison James's mind against Sir Walter.

At 2 o'clock in the morning on March 24, 1603, after three weeks of agonizing illness, Queen Elizabeth died, ending forty-four years and five months of a reign that still ranks as a high point in English history. As her final act, the dying queen named James as her successor. A delegation was sent to bring the new monarch to London, and on May 3 James arrived at Cecil's estate, Theobald's, outside London. Ralegh, in the West Country, hurried to welcome the new king. As Ralegh first met James, the Scot could not resist making a bad pun and greeted Ralegh with "Mon, I have heard 'rawly' of you!"

The contrast between the two men was startling. Although then more than fifty years old and crippled from the Cadiz battle, Ralegh was still an impressive man, well built, handsome, and beautifully attired. James appeared more of a buffoon than a monarch. As Lord David Cecil, a modern descendant of King James's host, Sir Robert Cecil, describes him,

nothing could have been more of a contrast to Queen Elizabeth than the thirty-eight-year-old James I, an awkward, ugly figure dressed in a shabby doublet heavily quilted to protect him from an assassin's dagger, with a straggly beard, a slobbering tongue too big for his mouth, who shambled about fiddling with his codpiece and . . . always leaning against something or someone to support a weight too heavy for his weak, knock-kneed legs. His talk was as unkingly as his looks: a garrulous stream in which out-of-the-way learning and long-winded theories mingled incongruously with homely endearments and jocular familiarities, all uttered in a broad Scottish accent.

This sounds like travesty, but it reflects honestly the private views of contemporaries, written only where they were not to be seen. The immaculate Ralegh must have instantly hated England's new monarch, but he had ample reason to fear this man who, for his pedantry and false scholarship, has earned the title "the wisest fool in Christendom."

Even before he left Theobald's to set foot in court, James struck at Ralegh: he withdrew the monopolies granted by Elizabeth, remov-

James VI of Scotland succeeded Elizabeth on the throne of England in 1603. Influenced by Robert Cecil and Henry Howard, earl of Northampton, James initiated a series of measures designed to deprive Ralegh of his property, remove him from court, and bring him to trial for treason. Engraving from copy in North Carolina Collection.

ing the source of Sir Walter's income. In mid-May he removed Ralegh as captain of the guard and gave the post to the man who had held that position at his Edinburgh court. And when, during the procession to London, the bishop of Durham requested the return of Durham House to him, James concurred and at the end of May ordered Ralegh to vacate the premises. In spite of protests, Ralegh could gain only an extension of time (to July 25) before moving all his servants and household effects to Sherborne, which was already overcrowded. In the same month, while attending the king during a hunt at Windsor Castle, Ralegh was called before the Privy Council for questioning. What did he know, he was asked, about plots "to surprise the King's person?" What private dealings had he had with the ambassador from the Spanish Netherlands? Sir Walter, taken completely by surprise, swore ignorance and innocence but was immediately placed under house arrest. In less than a week he was a prisoner in the Tower, charged with high treason and awaiting trial on charges of plotting "to deprive the King of his crown and dignity; to subvert the government, and alter the true religion established in England; and to levy war against the King." Because of the prevalence of the plague in London, Ralegh's trial was held before the Court of the King's Bench at Winchester on November 17, 1603.

The outcome was never in doubt: Ralegh was still hated by the populace for his putative role in the Essex affair, and the commission established by James to try him was comprised of his most violent enemies. No evidence other than hearsay testimony was presented; no examination of witnesses was permitted; accusations were accepted as fact. Yet, in spite of the hopelessness of the situation, Ralegh conducted himself with a gravity and charm that impressed his hearers. As Dudley Carlton, who was present, wrote to John Chamberlain, Sir Walter

answered with that temper, wit, learning, courage, and judgment, that save that it went with the hazard of his life, it was the happiest day that ever he spent. And so well he shifted all the advantages that were taken against him that were not "fama malum gravius quam res" and a ill name half hanged, in the opinion of all men he had been acquitted. . . . In one word, never was a man so hated and so popular in so short a time.

In spite of the favorable impression Sir Walter made, the final judgment was "guilty" and the penalty a traitor's death. Lord Grey and Lord Cobham were also charged and convicted. Executions were set for December, and Ralegh was moved to the Tower to await the hanging, drawing, and quartering he expected. At the last moment, possibly moved by the triviality of the evidence and after playing cat and mouse with his prisoners, James stayed the executions. All three prisoners remained convicted traitors but were permitted to live in the Tower "at the King's pleasure." Ralegh was given residence in two rooms on the second floor of the "Bloody Tower" and allowed to keep one

While imprisoned in the Tower of London, Ralegh attempted to overcome his physical restrictions through active study, reading, and writing. He continued to converse with visitors and to oversee his personal affairs. Engraving from copy in North Carolina Collection.

servant in attendance within and another to come and go to do his bidding outside. These confined quarters were to be his earthly residence for the remainder of his life, except for the brief period of his second voyage to Guiana.

Unlike most prisoners in the Tower, Ralegh, after the first flurry of fear and excitement, found escape through the freedom of his mind. To collect his thoughts and crystallize his ideas required time and leisure, both of which he had in plenty. Although he had lost most of his income with his attainder, he still managed his affairs in some detail from the Tower. His daily routine was diverse: he talked with his friends (the earl of Northumberland had joined him in the Tower following the exposure of the Gunpowder Plot of November, 1605, an attempt to blow up Parliament and assassinate King James and other government leaders), he bowled on the green, he gardened (he was still experimenting with plants brought back from America), he conducted experiments in chemistry (he had taken over the Tower lieutenant's henhouse for a laboratory), and he took his daily constitutional along the wall still known as "Ralegh's Walk." And, strangely enough, although he was a prisoner of the king, he became a close friend and personal adviser to James's wife, Queen Anne, and to Henry, the Prince of Wales. It was to instruct and advise James's first son and heir that he began seriously to write. And in true Ralegh fashion, he chose for his first major effort the largest subject possible to conceive: he set himself to the task of writing *The Historie of*

While confined in the Tower, Ralegh became a close personal friend and adviser to Henry, Prince of Wales, son of King James, as well as to James's wife, Queen Anne. Prince Henry and his mother attemped unsuccessfully to secure Sir Walter's release from imprisonment. Engraving from Lodge, *Portraits of Illustrious Personages*, IV.

the World, designed to begin with God's creation of the earth and to continue through the reign of Elizabeth.

Naturally such a task was beyond the scope of a single man—even Ralegh—and was never completed. But the quality, scope, and magnitude of the portion he did complete—a huge folio of six books that ends with the fall of the Macedonian kingdom in 168 B.C.—has ensured Sir Walter a place among the world's great writers of history. Its popularity can be seen in the fact that during the seventeenth century it went through eleven editions—more than the combined number of publications of Shakespeare, Jonson, Marlowe, and Spenser—and it is still read occasionally and quoted frequently.

It would not be right to say that Ralegh grew reconciled to life in the Tower or that he enjoyed his stay there. But, unlike most of the Tower prisoners, he did not give up to despair or spend his time in lamentations. He continued to keep abreast of what was going on; he felt a part of the life of his country; and he had the courage to offer advice to the statesmen with whom he had worked—even the king. The courage and vitality that marked his career from the beginning remained with him within the grim stone walls of England's greatest fortress.

XXIV. The Fatal Voyage: Guiana Revisited

In spite of his apparent adjustment to Tower life, Ralegh never forgot his dreams of wealth and colonial expansion in the New World. In this he was probably stimulated and prodded by Lawrence Keymis, who had been imprisoned in the Tower with him and who remained one of his closest associates. Keymis had declared in his *Second Voyage to Guiana* that "Myself and the remain[der] of my few years I have bequeathed whole to Raleana [as he called the Orinoco], and all my thoughts live only in that action." Ralegh, as a result, besieged James with plans for wresting the riches of Guiana away from the Spanish, and James (although he still distrusted Sir Walter) was, like Cecil, intrigued with the thought of quick riches. Ralegh was even more determined, since he saw Guiana as his only hope for release and possible fame and fortune. Both Prince Henry and Queen Anne were strong supporters and at the time of the prince's death in 1612 were striving to obtain Sir Walter's release. James approved additional voyages of exploration in the Orinoco region for Robert Harcourt in 1609 and Sir Thomas Roe the following year. Unfortunately for Ralegh, their reports were not highly favorable; they reported that the Spanish had enlarged their settlement near the Caroni and had strengthened the fort at San Thomé. Keymis and Ralegh could only argue that these actions proved the wealth of the nearby mines.

Meanwhile, James's dissipations and extravagances were catching up with him. A sensational scandal surrounding the murder of Sir Thomas Overbury in the Tower in 1613 rocked the court. The sordid details presented at the trial revealed a rottenness within the royal circle and led to parliamentary demands for reform—demands reinforced by threats to refuse to levy taxes to support the throne. James was searching everywhere for money, and Ralegh pressed his case for a return to Guiana.

Cecil had died, alone and unloved, and James had chosen as a new favorite the handsome George Villiers, who was less opposed to Ralegh than Robert Carr, earl of Somerset and private secretary to James, had been. Henry Howard died shortly afterward, and it was then disclosed that both Cecil and Howard had long been in the pay of Spain and had accepted the pension they had accused Ralegh of taking. Ralegh's proposals impressed Sir Ralph Winwood, Cecil's successor as principal minister, and Villiers, the new favorite (rumor had it that Ralegh bribed them), to the effect that on March 16, 1616, over the strong objections of the Spanish ambassador, Count Gondomar, James released Ralegh from imprisonment and authorized him to make preparations for another voyage to Guiana.

The commission given by James to Sir Walter was much more restrictive than those issued by Elizabeth. Not only did the "trusty and well-beloved" phrase now read "under peril of the law," but it was given under the Privy Seal instead of the Royal Seal, and included were injunctions against harming any Spaniard that might be encountered under any circumstance. Under this commission the king was to receive all taxes and duties on anything Ralegh might bring back, plus one fifth of all the gold and silver, including ore. And, unbelievably, to counter the objections of Gondomar, King James secretly agreed to reveal to him complete information concerning Ralegh's plans, ships, men, armament, and schedules of departure and arrival. In short, James was giving Ralegh's expedition the kiss of death in advance.

Knowing that this voyage was his final possible chance for redemption, Ralegh immediately began to liquidate his remaining assets to finance this last venture. In this he was successful; even after thirteen years of disfavor and imprisonment, he raised nearly £30,000 in its support. Everything that money could buy—ships, supplies, maps, instruments—was purchased to ensure the success of his expedition. Phineas Pett of Deptford, the shipbuilder who had built the *Prince Royal,* was commissioned to build the flagship, a large warship of 500 tons, which was named, appropriately, the *Destiny.* A contemporary report dated March 15, 1617, which gives a "view and survey of such ships as were in the river Thames, ready to go to sea under the command of Sir Walter Ralegh . . . ," lists six warships and one pinnace, together totaling 1,215 tons and carrying 431 men and 121 pieces of ordnance.

For its day, this was a formidable fleet with considerable firepower and the quickness and maneuverability that had already beaten the Spanish war fleet in every encounter. There is some evidence that Ralegh was aware that King James had laid a trap for him: his cousin, Sir George Carew, wrote to their friend Roe in India that "the alarm of [Ralegh's] journey is flown into Spain and, as he tells me, sea forces are prepared to lie for him, but he is nothing appalled with the report, for he will be a good fleet and well manned."

The injunction against harming any Spaniard posed real problems. For a time Sir Walter urged the king to ally with France and let the French hold the Spanish at bay while he sailed to the mine and loaded his ships with ore. This James was unwilling to do. Rumors were abroad that the French had offered Ralegh a commission and safe harborage in French ports if he violated the king's injunctions, but no evidence exists to prove this.

It was not laxity in the physical preparations for the expedition that foredoomed it; once again it was human error—the error of Sir Walter's choice of people to be trusted with his final venture. The responsibility for the success or failure of the Guiana expedition rested with three people: Sir Walter himself; his beloved son and heir Walter (or Wat, as he was called); and Lawrence Keymis, his most trusted friend in Guiana affairs. The three men were embarking on an exacting and dangerous mission that required strength, daring, and judgment; instead, they displayed physical weakness and foolhardiness, and all perished as a result of personal inadequacies.

Ralegh began his mission boldly and piously. On May 3 he issued his famous orders to his fleet. Not only did he endorse the king's demands that no foreign soldier or citizen should be harmed; he also extended the king's orders to include full courtesy to the natives, proclaiming that "no man shall force any woman, be she Christian or heathen, upon pain of death." Gambling, stealing, and swearing were forbidden at all times; strict discipline and obedience to orders were required at all times; divine services were to be held twice daily, at sea or on land. It is difficult to believe that the crew (to which he later referred as "the scum of the earth") would have lived up to these standards, but Ralegh felt sure his authority would prevail over their inherent weaknesses.

The conscripts were not enthusiastic, however. They kept escaping almost as fast as they were recruited. An entire crew could disappear overnight, and a new one would have to be assembled. It was June 12, 1617, before Ralegh could raise his sails to move from Plymouth harbor, and already the weather had turned bad. Contrary winds blew his ships back into port. On the next tide they sailed again, and they were all blown back into Falmouth harbor. They set out a third time and were blown clear to the Scilly Islands, where a gale sank one of the pinnaces, resulting in the loss of all hands. The continuing winds and high seas, together with stale meat and overripe fruit, began to sicken the crews. None suffered more than Sir Walter, always a bad sailor, who was ill before his ships were out of sight of land. The gales blew them to Cork in southern Ireland, where Ralegh landed and visited his old friends in order to regain his strength. It was August 19, with the season well advanced, before the fleet departed Ireland for the Canaries, the first leg of their crossing, to provision for the long ocean journey to the Indies.

On their way to the Canaries, discipline started to break down. The small fleet encountered four French ships, and Captain John Bailey in the *Husband* captured the vessels as prizes. Ralegh objected: their license did not permit them to take French ships. It required all his strength to force their release, and the action disgruntled many of his men. At Lanzarote in the Canary Islands, a garrison, mistaking them for marauding Barbary pirates, fired on Ralegh's landing party and killed three of the crew. Once again it required Ralegh's full authority to quiet his officers and men and move them to a more friendly island. Captain Bailey was so incensed that he sailed the *Husband* back to England, where, to spite Ralegh, he reported that Sir Walter had turned to piracy. Count Gondomar made the most of this, reminding James that when Ralegh returned he was to be turned over to Spain for hanging. Only when other ships arrived with the true story did the sensation die down, and Bailey was imprisoned until he was willing to issue an abject apology.

But worse was to come. On September 24, while the ships sailed smoothly toward Guiana, the sickness that had struck earlier returned in full force. On the first day, fifty men on the *Destiny*, a quarter of the total, were completely incapacitated by a raging fever. Officers and men on the other vessels suffered the same illness, making it difficult to find men to stand watch or to man the sails. Off the Cape Verde Islands a hurricane struck, and one of the ships was lost. This was followed by an extreme calm and exceedingly high temperatures, which intensified the fever. Men were dying daily on all the ships; they were thrown overboard with no ceremony. The crossing became a nightmare, and it was not until November 12 that they finally arrived at the mouth of the Cayenne River in Guiana. There Ralegh's first act was to write to his wife:

Sweet heart,
I can yet write unto you but with a weak hand, for I have suffered the most violent calenture [tropical fever] for fifteen days that ever man did and lived; but God that gave me a good heart in all my adversities hath also

now strengthened it in the hell-fire of heat.

We have had two most grievous sicknesses in our ship, of which forty-two have died, and there are yet many sick; but having recovered the land of Guiana this 12 of November, I hope we shall recover them. We are yet two hundred men, and the rest of our fleet are reasonably strong—strong enough, I hope, to perform what we have undertaken.

Sir Walter finished his letter with pride:

To tell you that I might be here King of the Indians were a vanity, but my name hath still lived among them. Here they feed me with fresh meat, and all the country yields; all offer to obey me. . . .

Yet, in spite of this optimism, Ralegh's expedition was in difficulty and some replanning was necessary. Among those listed by Ralegh in his letter to Bess as having died during the crossing were his military commander, Captain John Piggott; his chief lieutenant; the master surgeon; the master refiner; the governor of the Bermudas; the provost marshal; and two of his own personal servants—Christopher Hammond and John Talbot. It was already clear that Ralegh himself, because of age and continuing infirmities, could not lead the expedition up the Orinoco or seek the mine upon which he was depending for his freedom.

A council of war was called, and Ralegh made several final decisions. Since neither he nor Sir Warham St. Leger, the son of a friend of Ralegh from the Irish wars who had volunteered to accompany Sir Walter, was well enough to lead the expedition, they would remain behind as a rear guard to protect against any following Spanish vessels. Five of the smaller vessels, which together carried 150 sailors and 250 soldiers, should proceed up the Orinoco to the mine area under direction of Lawrence Keymis, the only man who knew where they were going. George Ralegh, Sir Walter's nephew, was to be sergeant-major, and Wat Ralegh one of his captains. Orders were clear: the forces were to go upriver to the Caroni juncture, making no offensive move against any Spaniards they might encounter at San Thomé or the Spanish fortifications. From the Caroni they were to move overland to the mine. If attacked by the Spanish, they were to defend themselves only. Once the mine was reached, they were to remove as much ore as they could carry, or, if under attack, at least enough to prove the wealth of the ore upon their return. If worse came to worst and the Spanish waged all-out war, they were to defend themselves to the best of their ability. Ralegh put all his trust in his leaders but had little confidence in his conscripts. As he told Keymis, "I know, a few gentlemen excepted, what a scum of men you have, and I would not, for all the world, receive a blow from the Spaniards to the dishonor of our nation."

There exist many reports as to exactly what happened during the Orinoco visit, but they are so contradictory that they have been interpreted many ways. Historians are divided: some assert that both Ralegh and Keymis knew there was no mine and that the attack on San Thomé was a diversionary tactic; some believe Keymis's report that the Spanish had moved their settlement downstream twenty miles, causing the English to come upon it unawares and to become unwittingly forced into battle; others hold that the Spanish attacked the English, who merely defended themselves. But to most readers who examine the testimony that remains, the most reliable evidence appears to be that of Ralegh himself.

Three main sources of information about the Guiana venture from Ralegh's point of view remain: (1) his log or journal of the voyage from the departure from Cork to February 13, 1618 (when he received in a letter from Keymis notice of the death of Wat and life suddenly became meaningless); (2) the defense of his actions, which he composed in England after his return to counter the rumors and charges levied against him; and (3) the letters he wrote during the course of the action. These are serious documents, convincingly written, internally consistent. They are the thoughts of a man, old and feeble in body but still vigorous and determined in spirit, who believed in a rich mine of gold and silver somewhere near the Caroni River and the San Thomé garrison; who thought the Spanish would permit the English to dig for ore; and who was confident that Keymis would lead the expedition reasonably and according to his orders. Sir Walter realized that many things could go wrong, but he had by no means lost faith in the New World and in the contribution it could make to the enrichment and aggrandizement of the England he devotedly loved.

After dispatching his river boats, there was little for Ralegh to do but keep an eye out for Spanish vessels and wait for news. Shortly after seeing five small boats off from the Cayenne River, he moved his fleet to Puncto Gallo, their appointed rendezvous, to survey the site and assess its defenses. At the end of December, 1617, he moved north and anchored about ten leagues from a Spanish settlement, where he hoped to get fresh fruit and meat for his still-fevered associates. In mid-January, 1618, he sent Sir John Fern to trade, but Fern and the men accompanying him were fired on and withdrew. Later that month the Spanish ambushed an English work party engaged in boiling pitch for caulking. Ralegh and St. Leger pursued the Spanish, who escaped into the forest. On February 1 Sir Walter's party captured a troop of seven Indians who gave Ralegh some unsettling news from upstream. As he wrote in his journal:

one of them . . . told me that certain Indians of the drowned lands . . . told him that the English in Orinoco had taken St. Thome, slain Diego de Palmita, slain Capt. Erenta and Capt. John Rues, and that the rest of the Spaniards (their Captains slain) fled into the mountains, and that two English Captains were also slain. This tale was also confirmed by another Indian which my men brought from the Indian town. . . .

Five days later, Ralegh, anxious for news, "sent a skiff over toward the Orinoco manned with 10 musketeers to hear what was become of my men there." On February 13, before they could report, the journal closes without explanation. A letter from Keymis containing news that Sir Walter knew meant the end of all his hopes and aspirations had arrived.

Keymis's letter, followed shortly by his account in person, told a dismal and devastating story. For some reason, instead of going past San Thomé to the entrance of the Caroni as planned, Keymis had landed his troops on the south bank (the same side as the town and fort) about three miles downstream from the settlement. The ships proceeded to a position opposite the fort, where they were fired upon but held their fire, remaining just out of range. The soldiers, meanwhile, were indecisively discussing their courses of action—whether to attack or to go around the settlement. As darkness descended, the men, "ready to repose themselves for the night," were suddenly assaulted from the woods. The unexpected fury of the attack caused brief panic, and it appeared there might be considerable loss of life. But a few of the captains, most notably young Wat Ralegh, rallied their men to counterattack into the forest. Almost before they knew it, the English came out into a clearing to find themselves facing the governor and soldiers ready to defend the town. Again there was hesitation, but Captain Ralegh with characteristic impetuousity sprang forward crying, according to all accounts, "Come on my hearts!" A volley was fired, and Ralegh's son was dead.

According to the report of one Captain Parker, another Englishman present,

The death in 1618 of Ralegh's son Wat was a crushing blow to his father, who wrote that with the loss of his son "all respect of the world hath taken end in me." This painting of Sir Walter and Wat was made at an earlier date, when Wat was a young boy. Photograph from copy in North Carolina Collection.

We lost Captain Ralegh and Captain Cosmor, but Captain Ralegh lost himself with his unadvised daringness. . . . Captain Cosmor led the forlorn hope with some 50 men, after him I brought up the first division of shot, next brought up Captain Ralegh a division of pikes, who no sooner heard us charged but indiscreetly came from his command to us, where he was unfortunately welcomed with a bullet which gave him no time to call for mercy to our heavenly father for his sinful life he had led. . . .

The remainder of the expedition was a fiasco. Keymis made a half-hearted effort to ascend the Caroni, only to lose more men from the constant firing from the wooded shores. Rejoining the ships, Keymis's men continued upstream, going farther inland than any Englishman had ever been—300 miles, according to the Spanish, 120 according to Keymis. But all the way they were under constant attack, and it seems obvious that Keymis was only putting off the evil day of returning to face Ralegh. After twenty-nine days, the men returned to San Thomé. They tried to parley with the enemy: they put out white flags, but the Spanish maintained their guerrilla warfare. Keymis, with only 150 men left of the 400 with whom he started, at last burned the city and turned downstream to make his final rendezvous with the man whom he had failed—and to add his own life to the long roster of those sacrificed in the search for the fabled gold of El Dorado.

Ralegh had suffered more than he could bear. The death of Wat meant the end of all his dreams of family, fame, and fortune. In the bitterness of his despair, he addressed a letter to Sir Ralph Winwood, King James's secretary of state, not knowing that Winwood had died on the very day that Ralegh had first been stricken with the virulent fever. This letter comes from Sir Walter's heart and illuminates the entire Guiana venture from his own point of view. The letter, written from St. Christophers, one of the islands of the Antilles, and bearing the date March 21, 1618, reads:

Sir,
    As I have not hitherto given you any account of our proceedings and passage toward the Indes, so have I no other subject to write of since our arrival than of the greatest and sharpest misfortunes that have ever befallen any man: for whereas, for the first, all those that navigate between Cape Verde and America do pass it in 15 or 20 days at most, we found the winds so contrary (which is also contrary to nature), and so many violent storms and rains, as we spent six weeks in that passage, by reason whereof and that in so great heat we wanted water (for at the Isle Bravo off Cape Verde we lost our cables and anchors and our water casks; being driven from the Island with a hurricane and were all like to have perished) great sickness fell amongst us and carried away great numbers of our ablest men, both

for sea and land. The 17 of November we had sight of the coast of Guiana, and soon after came to anchor in five degrees at the river Caliana [Cayenne]. Here we stayed till the 4th of December, landed our sick men, set up the barges and shallops which we brought out of England in quarters, washed our ships, and took in fresh water, being fed and assisted by the Indians of my old acquaintance, with a great deal of love and respect.

Myself, having been in the hands of Death, without hope, some six weeks (and not yet able otherwise to move than as I was carried in a chair) gave order to five small ships to sail into Orinoco, having Captain Keymis for their conductor towards the mine; and in those five ships five companies of fifty, under the command of Captain Parker and Captain North, brothers to the Lord Mounteagle and the Lord North, valiant gentlemen, and of infinite patience for the labor, hunger, and heat which they have endured. My son had the third company; Captain Thornix of Kent the fourth; Captain Chudley, by his lieutenant, the fifth. But as my Sergeant-Major, Captain Pigott of the Low Countries, died in the former miserable passage, so my Lieutenant, Sir Warham St. Leger, lay sick without hope of life, and the charge conferred on my nephew, George Ralegh, who had also served long with singular commendations in the Low Countries, but by reason of my absence and of Sir Warham's, was not well obeyed as the enterprise required.

As they passed up the river, the Spaniards began the war and shot at us, both with their ordnance and muskets, whereupon the company were forced to charge them, and soon after beat them out of their town. In the assault whereof my son (having more desire of honor than of safety) was slain, and with whom, to say the truth, all respect of the world hath taken end in me. And although these five Captains had as weak companies as ever followed valiant leaders, yet were there amongst them some 20 or 30 very adventurous gentlemen and of singular courage, as of my son's company, Mr. Knevet, Mr. Hammon, Mr. Langworth, Mr. John Plessington, his officers; Sir John Hamden, Mr. Simon Leak (corporal of the field), Mr. Hammon's elder brother, Mr. Nicholas of Buckingham, Mr. Roberts of Kent, Mr. Perin, Mr. Tresham, Mr. Mullineaux, Mr. Winter and his brother, Mr. Wray, Mr. Miles Herbert, Mr. William Herbert, Mr. Bradshaw, Captain Hall, and others.

Sir, I set down the names of these gentlemen, to the end that if his Majesty shall have cause to use their service, it may please you to take knowledge of them for very sufficient men.

The other five ships stayed at Trinidad, having no other port capable of them near Guiana. The second ship was commanded by my vice-admiral, Captain John Pennington, of whom (to do him right) I must confess that he is one of the sufficientest gentlemen for the sea that England hath. The third, by Sir Warham St. Leger, an exceeding valiant and worthy gentleman. The fourth by Sir John Fern, and the fifth by Captain Chidley of Devon. With these five ships I daily attended the Armada of Spain, which, had they set upon us, our forces divided—the one half in Orinoco a hundred and fifty miles from us—we had not only been torn in pieces, but all those in the river had also perished, being of no defense at all for a sea fight; for we had resolved to have burnt by their sides, and to have died there, had the Armada arrived;

but belike they stay for us at Marguerita, by which they know we must pass towards the Indies.

For it pleased his Majesty to value us so little as to command me upon my allegiance, to set down under my hand the country and the very river by which I was to enter it; to set down the number of my men and burden of my ships; with what ordnance every ship carried; which being made known to the Spanish ambassador and by him, in post, sent to the King of Spain, a dispatch was made by him and his letters sent from Madrid before my departure out of the Thames; for his first letter, sent by a bark of advice, was dated the 19th of March, 1617, at Madrid; which letter I have here enclosed sent your Honor. The rest I reserve, not knowing whether these may be intercepted or not. The second, of the King's dated the 17 of May, sent also by a caravel to Don Diego de Palomeque, governor of Guiana, El Dorado, and Trinidad; the third by the Bishop of Puerto Rico and delivered to Palomeque the 15th of July at Trinidad; and the fourth was sent from the Farmer and Secretary of his Customs in the Indies at the same time. By that of the King's hand, brought by the Bishop, there was also a commission for the speedy levying of 300 soldiers and ten pieces of ordnance to be sent from Puerto Rico for the defense of Guiana; 150 from Nuevo Reino de Granada, under the command of Captain Antonia Musica, and the other 150 from Puerto Rico to be conducted by Captain Francesco Zanchio.

Now, Sir, if all that have traded to the Indies since his Majesty's time know it that the Spaniards have flayed alive those poor men which they have taken, being but merchantmen, what death and torment shall we expect if they conquer us? Certainly, they have hitherto failed grossly, being set out unto them as we were, and discovered, both for our numbers, time, and place.

Lastly, to make an apology for not working the mine, although I know not (his Majesty excepted) whom I am to satisfy so much as myself, having lost my son and my estate in the enterprise; yet it is true that the Spaniards took more care to defend the passages leading unto it, than they did their town, which (say the King's instructions) they might easily do, the country being 'aspera et fragosa'. But it is true that when Keymis found the rivers low and that he could not approach the banks in most places near the mine by a mile, and when he found a descent, a volley of muskets came from the woods upon the boat and slew two of the rowers, hurt six others, and shot a valiant gentleman, Captain Thornix, in the head, of which wound he hath languished to this day. He (to wit, Keymis) following his own advice that it was in vain to discover the mine (for he gave me this excuse at his return that the companies of English in their town of St. Thome were hardly able to defend it against the daily and nightly alarms and assaults of the Spaniards; that the passage to the mine was of thick and impassable woods; that being discovered, they had no men to work it), did not discover it at all. For it is true that the Spaniards, having two gold mines near the town—the one possessed by Pedro Rodrigo de Parana; the second, Hernian Fruntino; the third, of silver, by Francisco Fachardo—[had abandoned them] for the want of negroes to work them. For, as the Indians cannot be constrained, by a law of Charles the Fifth, so the Spaniards will not, nor can they endure the labor of these mines, whatsoever that braggadochio the Spanish ambassador, say: I shall prove it under the proprietary's [hand], the custom books, and by the King's quinto [fifth], of which I recovered an ingot or two. And I shall make it appear to any Prince or State that will undertake it, how easily those mines and five or six more may be possessed, and the most of them in those places which never yet have been attempted by any enemy, nor any passage to them discovered by the English, Dutch, or French.

But at Keymis's return from Orinoco, when I rejected his counsel and his course, and told him that he had undone me and wounded my credit with the King past recovery, he slew himself. For I told him that, seeing my son was lost, I cared not if he had lost a hundred [men] more in opening the mine, so my credit had been saved. For I protest before God, had not Captain Whitney (whom I gave more countenance unto than to all the captains of my fleet) run from me at the Granadas and carried another ship with him of Captain Wollaston's, I would have left my body at St. Thome by my son's, or have brought with me out of that or other mines so much gold ore as should have satisfied the King that I had propounded no vain thing.

What shall become of me now, I know not; I am unpardoned in England, and my poor estate consumed; and whether any other Prince or State will give me bread, I know not. I desire your Honor to hold me in your good opinion, and to remember my service to my Lords of Arundel and Pembroke; to take some pity on my poor wife, to whom I dare not write, for renewing the sorrow for her son; and beseech you to give a copy of these to my Lord Carew. For to a broken mind, to a weak body and weak eyes, it is torment to write many letters. I have found many things of importance for discovering the estate and weakness of the Indies which, if I live, I shall hereafter impart unto your Honor, to whom I shall ever remain a faithful servant,

Walter Ralegh

Obviously, Ralegh was nearly deranged as a result of his tragic experiences. The death of the son in whom he placed all his hopes, the betrayal of Keymis, who had made little or no effort to find the mine on which Ralegh's life and fortune depended, and the revelations concerning the king's letters of treachery, captured at San Thomé—these were greater griefs than even a great and courageous spirit like Sir Walter's could bear. Ralegh was bitter: he could not forgive those who caused his downfall and could not decide whether to return to England or to seek asylum elsewhere.

Rumors that Ralegh may have killed Keymis in anger persist to this day. Had he done so, he might have been forgiven by a more sympathetic generation. But he denied these accusations: although his cold rejection of Keymis might have caused Keymis to kill himself, Ralegh had taken no direct action against him. There is an attachment to the Winwood letter in the Cecil archives; it is either a postscript to the letter or a second note, written immediately after it and sent at the same time. It gives additional details concerning the death of Keymis:

Sir, since the death of Keymis, it is confessed by the Sergeant-Major and others of his inward friends, that he told them when they were at the [Caroni] river's mouth coming thence, that he could have brought them to the mine within two hours' march from the river's side; but because my son was slain, myself unpardoned and not like to live, he had no reason to open the mine either for the Spaniards or for the King. They answered that the King (though I were not pardoned) had granted me my patent under the great seal. He replied that the grant to me was to a man who was "non ens" in law, and therefore of no force. This discourse he had, which I knew not of till after his death. When I was resolved to write unto your Honor, he prayed me to join with him in excusing his not going to the mine. I answered him I would not do it; that if himself could satisfy the King and State that he had reason not to open it, I should be glad of it; but for my part, I must avow it that he knew it, and that he might, with little loss, have done it; other excuse I would not frame. He then told me that he would wait on me presently and give me better satisfaction. But I was no sooner come from him into my cabin, but I heard a pistol go off over my head, and sending up to know who shot it, word was brought that Keymis had shot it out of his cabin window to cleanse it; his boy going into the cabin, found him lying on his bed with much blood by him, and looking on his face, saw he was dead. The pistol being but little, the bullet did not crack his rib; but he, turning him over, found a long knife in his body, all but the handle.

Sir, I have sent into England in a fly-boat with my cousin Herbert (a very valiant and honest gentleman) divers other unworthy persons, good for nothing either by land or sea; and although it was at their own suit, I know that they will wrong me in all they can. I beseech your Honor that this scum of men may not be believed of me, who have taken more pain and suffered more than the meanest rascal in the ship. These being gone, I shall be able, if I live, to keep [to] the sea till the end of August, with four reasonably good ships.

Sir, whensoever God shall permit me to arrive in any part of Europe, I will not fail to let your Honor know what we have done. Till then, and ever,

Your Honor's servant, W. Ralegh.

On March 22, 1618, Ralegh summoned the courage to write to his wife. He began: "I was loathe to write because I knew not how to comfort you; and God knows I never knew what sorrow meant till now." His only comfort came from the stoic recollection that others, too, had suffered: "All I can say to you is that you must obey the will

121

and providence of God; and remember that the Queen's Majesty bore the loss of Prince Henry with a magnanimous heart, and the Lady Harrington of her only son." And with the prescience of deep grief, he concluded: "Comfort your heart, dearest Bess; I shall sorrow for us both. I shall sorrow the less, because I have not long to sorrow, because not long to live."

XXV. The Bitter Victory: Death

Seven months elapsed between the end of the Guiana voyage and Sir Walter Ralegh's beheading. These were days and weeks that seemed to Ralegh and to all those around him like the frenzied and irrational dreams of a troubled mind. Torn by grief over the loss of his son and despair at the end of his personal dreams of greatness, apprehensive over the reception he would receive in England when (and if) he returned, still weak from the fever that had racked his body for months, fearful of the effects his anticipated death might have on his wife and friends, Ralegh was literally almost out of his wits, totally unable to decide what his proper course of action should be. In these final days, he was not the self-assured, confident, rational, and motivated man he had been since youth; he was, rather, vacillating and emotionally unstable, a victim of circumstances with no real control of his actions.

The end was inevitable. James could not pardon his old enemy, especially since Ralegh had not returned with the wealth he had promised in return for his release. Nor could he put any confidence in the "old fox," who was casting all possible wiles and stratagems to confuse the picture of his activities. Ralegh had sunk to many modes of deception in his near-madness. He had negotiated with the French about the possibility of landing on their soil rather than that of England and had returned to England only to save the bonds put up for him by his friends. Later, he had painted spots on his face and feigned sickness in order to gain time to prepare his own record of what happened on the Orinoco. Ralegh was fully aware that his return to Plymouth assured his doom. When, in mid-July, 1618, he and Bess started from Plymouth for London, he was quickly taken into custody and returned to the Tower in disgrace. There was much discussion in the inner circles of the court as to whether Sir Walter should be sent to Spain for trial and execution, but on October 15 word came from Madrid that King Philip III had decided that James should have the execution in England.

Three days later, Attorney General Sir Edward Coke presented James with the recommendations of a special commission appointed to determine how Sir Walter should be charged. A preliminary hearing was held on October 22, and Ralegh was informed of the charges against him. Although he defended his actions with reason, eloquence, and dignity, his testimony was unheeded and Sir Francis Bacon, newly appointed as lord chancellor, informed Ralegh that he must die.

It is interesting to note that in spite of all the Spanish charges and countercharges, the commission was unable to find any fatal flaw in the way Ralegh had conducted himself during the Guiana campaign. Although his men had burned the Spanish settlement at San Thomé, this could be excused on the grounds that Guiana was in reality English soil by virtue of Ralegh's having claimed it for Elizabeth during his earlier visit. This claim the commission was reluctant to deny. Ralegh could be said to have been repelling enemies, not attacking them. Nor could any charges of privateering be upheld. Since no new charges could be levied, it was finally decided that the simplest solution was for the king to withdraw his mercy from the death penalty that had been proclaimed in 1603 and to execute Ralegh as a traitor in accordance with that decree. James willingly accepted his withdrawal of mercy, but in so doing he nevertheless demonstrated his generous nature: Ralegh should not be subjected to the horrors of hanging, drawing, and quartering normally accorded to treasonable subjects but should instead be granted the mercy of the ax. The execution, James decided, should be carried out early in the morning following the final hearing—the festive Lord Mayor's Day, when crowds would be assembled in the eastern part of London, far from Westminster Palace in the west, where the execution would take place. James then took his court out of London, where no last-minute petitions for mercy could reach him.

Final hearing came on October 28, 1618, before the King's Bench at Westminster. During this critical period, Ralegh again suffered from alternate fits of fever and ague, lingering effects of his tropical disease. Although he could scarcely walk, he was led from the Tower across the breadth of London, past Durham House and its happier memories, to the palace. London citizens thronged the streets to view the limping old man, and, according to reports, the crowd, recognizing the importance of the event, was hushed and solemn. This final hearing was designed only for sentencing, but after some preliminary remarks, the attorney general could not refrain from a final comment: "Sir Walter Ralegh hath been a statesman, and a man who in regard of his parts and quality is to be pitied. He hath been a star at which the world hath gazed. But stars may fall, nay, must fall when they trouble the sphere wherein they abide." He then solemnly pronounced the sentence of death for early the next morning.

Ralegh spent the evening until after midnight with Bess, trying to console her and giving advice on how to handle her affairs. The Reverend Robert Tounson, a royal chaplain and dean of Westminster, assigned to instruct Ralegh in his last hours, found himself being instructed by Sir Walter. Ralegh's meeting with death showed the true mettle of the man. During this final day, when Sir Walter the man was closing his earthly existence, was born the legendary Sir Walter, who has captured the imagination of all later generations.

In a sense, Ralegh was glad it was over, and it must be said that he truly welcomed his release from earth. Dean Tounson wrote: "He was the most fearless of death that ever was known, and the most resolute and confident, yet with reverence and conscience." And Sir Dudley Carlton, a diplomat, said simply, "His happiest hours were those of his arraignment and execution." Even now, more than three and a half centuries later, it can be seen that it was Ralegh's death that gave full dimension to his active and fruitful life and luster to the whole world of Elizabethan England.

The most graphic firsthand account of Ralegh's last hours is found in the letter John Chamberlain, a writer of newsletters, wrote to Sir Dudley Carlton two days after the event. Chamberlain, evidently a witness at the scene, wrote:

I remember that in my last letter I said that Sir Walter Ralegh was not secure, but now he is past all peradventure, for upon Thursday morning he was beheaded in the old palace at Westminster 'twixt the Parliament House and the Church. . . . He was willing to prepare himself, and so was delivered to the sheriffs of London and conveyed to the Gatehouse [prison], where he spent the rest of the day in writing letters to the King and others, and in prayer with the Dean of Westminster who came the next morning at five o'clock and ministered to him the communion. And when he had broken his fast about eight o'clock, came to the scafford, where he found the Earls of Arundel, Oxford, Northampton, the Lord of Doncaster, and divers others. He made a speech of more than half an hour in which he cleared himself. . . . Then that he never had any ill intent toward His Majesty, not so much as in thought, [and] that he had no other pretense nor end in his last voyage [to Guiana] than the enriching of the King, the realm, himself, and his followers. . . . He confessed himself the greatest sinner that he knew, and no marvel, as having been a soldier, a seaman, and a courtier.

It will not be amiss to set down some few passages of divers that I have heard. The morning that he went to execution, there was a cup of excellent sack brought him, and being asked how he liked it, "As the fellow," said he, "that drinking of St. Giles bowl on the way to Tyburn, said it was a good drink if a man could tarry at it." As he went from Westminster Hall to the Gatehouse, he spied Sir Hugh Beeston in the throng, and calling to him prayed he would see him die tomorrow. Sir Hugh, to make sure work, got a letter from Secretary Lake to the sheriff to see him placed conveniently, and meeting them as they came near the scaffold, delivered his letter. But the sheriff by mishap had left his spectacles at home and put the letter in his pocket. In the meantime, Sir Hugh being thrust by, Sir Walter bade him farewell and said, "I know not what shift you will make, but I am sure to have a place." When the hangman asked him forgiveness, he desired to see the axe, and feeling the edge said it was a fair, sharp medicine to cure him of all his diseases and miseries. When he was laid down, some found fault that his face was westward and would have him turned. Whereupon rising, he said it was no great matter which way a man's head stood, so his heart lay right. He had given orders to the executioner that after some short meditation, when he stretched his hands, he should dispatch him. After once or twice putting forth his hands, the fellow (out of timorousness or some other cause) forebearing, he was fain to bid him "Strike!". And so at two blows he took off his head, though he stirred not a whit after the first. The people were much affected by the sight, insomuch that one was heard say that we had not another such head to cut off. . . .

His execution was the more remarkable in that it fell out the day of the Lord Mayor's triumph, though it began with a tragedy, and being a reasonably fair morning, grew very foul all the day after. . . .

Following Ralegh's execution, a sheet in his hand was found in his Bible, apparently written on the night before his death. The first six lines were a slightly revised version of a love poem he had written years before in happier days, when he was favored by the queen:

> Even such is Time! who takes in trust
> Our youth, our joys, and all we have,
> And pays us but with earth and dust:
> Who in the dark and silent grave,
> When we have wandered all our ways,
> Shuts up the stories of our days.

To this Sir Walter had added a final couplet:

> But from that earth, that grave, that dust,
> The Lord shall raise me up, I trust.

Notes

[1]A. L. Rowse, *Sir Walter Raleigh: His Family and Private Life* (New York: Harper and Brothers, 1962), 130-131.

[2]Maps, directions to various ports, sketched profiles of the land, etc., collected and highly prized by sailors.

[3]Abraham Cocke, captain of the *Hopewell*.

[4]Edward Spicer, captain of the *Moonlight*.

[5]High sand dunes, now eroded, that stood south of Port Ferdinando between present-day Rodanthe and Salvo on the Outer Banks.

[6]Francis Sparrow was captured later that year by Spaniards and taken to Spain as a prisoner; after some years he escaped and made his way back to England. Hugh Goodwin, through the help of the natives, escaped the Spanish and was still living at Morequito when Ralegh returned in 1617, having by then almost totally forgotten his native tongue.

Suggested Reading

On the Life of Sir Walter Ralegh

Because his complex character can be interpreted in many ways, Sir Walter Ralegh has always been a popular figure for biographers. Even at the present time it is not uncommon for two or three biographies to appear in a single year. This list, therefore, represents only a few of the volumes that might be consulted, and which have interested and stimulated the author.

Adamson, J. H., and H. F. Folland. *The Shepherd of the Ocean: An Account of Sir Walter Ralegh and His Times.* Boston: Gambit, Inc., 1969.

Edwards, Edward, *The Life of Sir Walter Ralegh. Based on Contemporary Documents. Together with His Lettters, Now First Collected.* London: Macmillan, 2 volumes, 1868. Old, but still a standard in many ways.

Fecher, Constance. *The Last Elizabethan: A Portrait of Sir Walter Ralegh.* New York: Farrar, Straus, and Giroux, 1972.

Lacey, Robert. *Sir Walter Ralegh.* New York: Athenaeum, 1974.

Rowse, A. L. *Sir Walter Ralegh, His Family and Private Life.* New York: Harper and Brothers, 1962.

Wallace, Willard Mosher. *Sir Walter Raleigh.* Princeton, N.J.: Princeton University Press, 1959.

Williams, Norman Lloyd. *Sir Walter Ralegh.* Philadelphia: Dufour Editions, 1963.

On Explorations and the New World

Only in recent years, with the study of new materials in the archives of Spain and Portugal, is the real picture of early exploration and settlement in the New World becoming clearer. The following works provide interesting insights into Ralegh's aspirations and activities with regard to such affairs.

Clapp, Henry. *With Raleigh to British Guiana.* London: Frederick Muller, Ltd., 1965.

Durant, David N. *Ralegh's Lost Colony.* London: Widenfeld and Nicolson, 1981.

Harlow, Vincent Todd. *The Discoverie of the large and bewtiful empire of Guiana, by Sir Walter Ralegh, edited from the original text, with introduction, notes and appendixes of hitherto unpublished documents. . . .* London: Argonaut Press, 1928.

_____ . *Ralegh's last voyage; being an account drawn out of contemporary letters and relations, both Spanish and English, of which the most part are now for the first time made public, concerning the voyage of Sir Walter Ralegh, knight, to Guiana in the year 1617 and the fatal consequences of the same.* London: Argonaut Press, 1932.

Kupperman, Karen Ordahl. *Roanoke, the Abandoned Colony.* New York: Rowman and Allenheld, 1984.

Quinn, David Beers. *New American World: A Documentary History of North America to 1612.* New York: Arno Press, 5 volumes, 1979. A collection of the contemporary documents that are presently illuminating this age of discovery. Selected by the outstanding modern authority in the field.

_____ . *North America from Earliest Discovery to First Settlements: The Norse Voyages to 1612.* New York: Harper and Row, 1977. An excellent brief survey of the entire period.

_____ . *Raleigh and the British Empire.* London: English Universities Press, second edition, 1962.

_____ . *The Roanoke Voyages, 1584-1590: Documents to Illustrate the English Voyages to North America under the Patent Granted to Walter Raleigh in 1584.* London: The Hakluyt Society, 2 volumes, 1955. A masterly work that includes all the important contemporary documents concerning the earliest American colonies.

Stick, David. *Roanoke Island: The Beginnings of English America.* Chapel Hill: University of North Carolina Press, 1983.